ISSUES IN MARXIST PHILOSOPHY

Volume III

EPISTEMOLOGY, SCIENCE, IDEOLOGY

ISSUES IN MARXIST PHILOSOPHY

Volume III
EPISTEMOLOGY, SCIENCE, IDEOLOGY

EDITED BY
JOHN MEPHAM
AND
DAVID-HILLEL RUBEN

HUMANITIES PRESS

First published in the United States in 1979 by
HUMANITIES PRESS INC.,
Atlantic Highlands, New Jersey 07716

© The Harvester Press Limited, 1979

Library of Congress Cataloging in Publication Data

Main entry under title:
Issues in Marxist philosophy.
  (Marxist theory and contemporary capitalism)
  CONTENTS: v. 1. Dialectics and method. – v.
  2. Materialism. – v. 3. Epistemology, science, ideology.
  1. Dialectical materialism – Addresses, essays,
  lectures. 2. Marx, Karl, 1818–1883 – Addresses, essays,
  lectures. 3. Historical materialism – Addresses, essays,
  lectures. I. Mepham, John, 1938– II. Ruben,
  David-Hillel. III. Series.
  B809.8.I774 1979   146'.3   79–12173

  ISBN 0-391-01020-4 (v. 3)
  ISBN 0-391-01021-2 pbk.

Photosetting by Thomson Press (India) Ltd., New Delhi
and printed in Great Britain by
Redwood Burn Limited, Trowbridge and Esher

Contents

Notes on Authors: Volume III

ROY EDGLEY had a working-class socialist childhood. He was academically trained in, and has taught, analytical philosophy, but is now working on socialist philosophy. He is Professor of Philosophy at the University of Sussex. He has contributed articles to *Radical Philosophy*, is the author of *Reason in Theory and Practice* and editor of the series *Philosophy Now* published by Harvester Press. He was declared 'unfit' to teach, by a national British newspaper in June 1973.

DEREK SAYER was born in 1950. He has a BA in Sociology from Essex University and a PhD from Durham University. He has been a Senior Research Fellow at the University of Durham and is at present Lecturer in Sociology at the Glasgow College of Technology. He has published articles in *Radical Philosophy*, *Sociological Review*, and *Sociology*, and is the author of *Marx's Method* (1979) and co-author of *Socialist Construction and Marxist Theory* (1978) and *For Mao* (1978).

ANDREW COLLIER was born in London in 1944. He studied philosophy at Bedford College and University College, London. He has taught philosophy at the Universities of Warwick and Sussex and is at present Lecturer in Philosophy at University College of North Wales, Bangor. His main philosophical interests are in issues raised by the human sciences, and in particular by the theories of Marx and Freud. He has published articles in *Radical Philosophy* and is author of *R. D. Laing : The Philosophy and Politics of Psychotherapy* (1977). He has been a member of the International Socialists and the Socialist Workers' Party since 1973.

ROY BHASKAR was born in London, studied at the University of Oxford and is at present a Lecturer in Philosophy at the University of Edinburgh. He is the author of *A Realist Theory of Science* and of a forthcoming work on the philosophy of social science, *The Possibility of Naturalism*. He is currently working on the philosophical implications of Marxism.

JOHN MEPHAM studied biochemistry at Oxford and the history and philosophy of science at Princeton. He has taught philosophy at the University of Sussex and at Reed College in Oregon. He has published articles on Aristotle, Van Helmont, Lévi-Strauss, Althusser and Marx. Since resigning from university teaching in 1976 he has worked as a translator (of Koyré, Gorz, Jakobson and Foucault) and as an editor. He was a member of the Brighton Labour Process Group of the Conference of Socialist Economists. His main intellectual interest is now in the poetics of the novel and he wrote 'Figures of Desire: Narration and Fiction' in *To the Lighthouse*' for G. D. Josipovici (ed.), *The Modern English Novel* (1976). He is at present writing about poetics and the modern French novel with a grant from the South East Arts Association.

STEVE BUTTERS studied at the Centre for Contemporary Cultural Studies at Birmingham University, and is at present working at the Institute for the Study of Drug Dependence in London.

KATHRYN RUSSELL is a doctoral candidate in philosophy at the University of Cincinnati. She received her BA from that university in 1973 and her MA in 1975. Her main philosophical interests are metaphysics, epistemology and Marxist philosophy of science. Her dissertation is on radical social science and the problem of ideology.

General Introduction

THE essays in these Volumes on issues in Marxist philosophy are all by authors from English-speaking countries. With only three exceptions, they are printed here for the first time. In these countries, Marxist philosophers have had to struggle over the years, reading and evaluating the works of important continental European philosophers, both Marxists and non-Marxists, and of questioning our own distance from them. We asked what specific contributions our relations to various English-speaking philosophical traditions can make to the advancement of Marxist philosophy, philosophical traditions to which we are essentially related even when the character of that relation is in many fundamental ways a critical one. Much Marxist philosophical writing in the English-speaking world over the last decade has been more or less confined to exegesis and assimilation of continental philosophical systems, Sartre and the Frankfurt School, Lukacs and Korsch, Gramsci and della Volpe, and more recently Althusser, Colletti, and Timpanaro. It will be clear to the reader of these present Volumes that these philosophers have exerted an important influence on their contents. These essays are not written in defiant ignorance or xenophobic dismissal of the work of these philosophers; on the contrary, we respect them by our attention to what they can teach us and by an attempt to make our own distinctive contribution to Marxist philosophy.

Thus, we think the time is ripe for going beyond the rather passive assimilation of continental European philosophy that has hitherto dominated the Marxist intellectual landscape in the English-speaking world. Many English-speaking philosophers are ready to make their own contributions in areas of philosophical discussion in which, in spite of the volume of writing produced by French, German, and Italian Marxist philosophers, debate is still in the utmost confusion. Many of us have the sense that the philosophical argument has not been nearly deep enough, has not made sufficiently deep contact with the really fundamental philosophical issues, and the Marxist positions on central philosophical issues are still quite crude and superficial. Very often, argument and discussion have not been pursued at sufficiently abstract level, or with sufficient persistence and tenacity. Sometimes Marxist philosophers write as if they must select one of a small number of possible answers to some central issue or difficulty, without exploring all the possible options or alternatives. Marxist philosophy can only advance if it reaches down to the most general and abstract of philosophical categories, by the methods of sustained, persistent discussion and rational argument. English-speaking philosophers have a distinctive role to play here and we hope that these Volumes of essays will show this.

These essays are not written by a group of philosophers who in any sense constitute a school setting up a new system of doctrine, a new catechism of truths, let alone reviving any old ones, although they are all written from within a classical Marxist orientation. Two of the essays were written more or less directly under the influence of Althusser, although they are very selective in what they take from his work and are not at all expositions of Althusserian positions. In many of the other essays, the figures of Althusser, Lukacs, Colletti, and Timpanaro appear as worthy opponents, and an attempt is made to open up discussion in a way that is distinctive and which draws more on the English-speaking philosophical virtues of disciplined argument and attention to detailed elaboration and defence of one's own positions.

Overall, a certain coherence of direction emerges from these essays. The reader will notice, first, the persistent appearance of realist categories (potentiality, natural or physical necessity, natural kinds, essence and appearance), some of which derive from the Aristotelian tradition, and all of which indicate, negatively, the deeply non-empiricist or non-positivist ontology and epistemology that dominates these volumes. Marxist philosophy, since its inception, has been driven between the Scylla of positivism and the Charybdis of idealism (usually of a 'humanist' variety). On the one side were figures such as Plekhonov, Engels, Dietzgen, Lenin, Bogdanov, and many writers of the period of the Second International; on the other, stood Lukacs, Deborin, the Frankfurt School, Korsch, Sartre, and various 'humanist' Marxist tendencies. Some, from the Austro-Marxists to Colletti, could think of no better way out of this impasse than the slogan 'back to Kant'. Now, there is no doubt that, with the passage of time, some of the specific concepts or doctrines propounded in these pages may be found to be problematic, or untrue to any authentic Marxism, in ways now hidden from their authors. What is distinctive in these essays, though, is their attempt to think through a Marxist philosophy in which Marxism is neither collapsed into a variety of positivism, nor into a version of idealism, nor is reduced to a footnote to *The Critique of Pure Reason*. Whatever historically limited validity any specific set of doctrines or ideas herein propounded may possess, these essays are important in a much less limited way for the authentic Marxism towards which they attempt to move. They do not try to wed Marxism to current intellectual fashion. They do not say that Marxism is 'really' Hegelian, or Kantian, or Aristotelian, or structuralist, or humanist. Marxism is distinctive, and these essays are distinctive just in so far as they attempt to characterize that distinctiveness. In most of the essays, empiricism is the main enemy, but this anti-empiricism is based on a serious examination of ontological questions which is rooted in different categories from the currently fashionable anti-empiricist Marxism of Althusser, or Colletti or Timpanaro. There is an insistence that the problems of defining dialectical materialist thought and method can only be undertaken seriously by an examination of the ontological categories of physical necessity and via an elimination of the empiricist notion of causality.

A related common theme is the insistence on the need for a re-emphasis of the importance of materialism and on the necessity for a realist theory of science. The work of Roy Bhaskar (*A Realist Theory of Science*, 1978) has been very influential in this area of discussion and we hope that one of the effects of these books might be to encourage the development of Marxist philosophy in directions which his work, as well as recent work by Ted Benton (*Philosophical Foundations of the Three Sociologies*, 1977) and Russell Keat and John Urry

(*Social Theory as Science*, 1975), have opened up. In both these first two common lines of development, there is also a realist insistence by many of the authors on how absolutely crucial it is to distinguish between ontology and epistemology. So much of the confusion and the unacceptable philosophical implications of recent British Althusserian writing can be traced back to the absence of this distinction, or to the inadequacy with which it is worked through. Indeed, some of that writing is naive enough to pose the explicit abandonment of epistemology, or ontology, or both. Many of the essays in these volumes single out the work of what we might call the British post-Althusserian idealists (especially Hindess and Hirst) as targets for attack, for their work is regarded as, at one and the same time, rather influential and philosophically extremely confused. In this sense, these volumes can be seen as an attempt to intervene in the general Marxist philosophical culture, especially of Britain and Australia, in an effort negatively to combat a specific, dominant, influential body of work and more positively to open up lines of research which we believe will prove much more useful.

Another feature of Marxist theoretical culture which requires critical attention is a certain common style of polemical writing. All too often, much of Marxist theoretical discussion has been marked by the method of 'impugning your opponent's credentials'. Frequently, the fixing of labels has replaced rational argument in these ongoing debates. Simply calling one's opponents 'idealist', 'positivist', 'empiricist', 'mechanical materialist', or 'Kantian', is apparently all that is required in order to discredit their views. When all else fails, the accusation of failing to carry on the class struggle in philosophy (something allegedly done by those who do not accept the accuser's favourite version of Marxism) proves to be a sure winner. Much of the responsibility for this style of argument can be attributed to those Marxist philosophers whose work is insufficiently flexible and undogmatic. Indeed, it is the inflexibility and lack of openness of their views at any one time which leads to the subsequent recantations and auto-critiques rather than the organic growth and development of their positions. Whether intentionally or not, this gives rise to little bands of disciples whose function is to memorize slogans as answers to questions of which they in fact have very little understanding. In the hands of such people, Marxist philosophy has seemed closed rather than open, rigid rather than alive and changing. Among such disciples, especially those of British Althusserianism, abstract, critical thought has often been replaced by complicated technical jargon, whose effect has been numbing rather than the stimulation of clear, precise argument, free from inflexibility, rigidity, and dogmatism. Pat phrases and well-rehearsed slogans have prevailed; repetition and textual exegesis have become the hallmarks of a tradition no longer alive because no longer critical of itself. Each disciple followed his master in every new twist and turn from Marxism and back again, through every period of auto-critique. One could even learn slogans to explain why previous slogans were now to be considered erroneous. Without ceasing to be polemical in the best sense, these present essays are attempts at rational, argumentative, critical thought; they attempt to arrive at justified and well-supported conclusions by the method of Marx and Engels themselves, the method of critical analysis and argument, open to the possibilities of its own fallibility and limitations. In brief, these essays display that undogmatic and flexible character that has always characterized Marxist thinking at its best.

Two more remarks seem in order in this general introduction to these volumes. First, we hope that they will be read not only by philosophers but also by the many Marxists and non-Marxists who are troubled by the questions that are dealt with here. For example, many economists, engaged in difficult discussions about the concept of value and its status, have sensed the need for philosophical literature on the underlying problems of dialectical method and the theory of science. Many biologists and psychologists find that questions about the *materiality* of the objects of their study are directly raised by their own scientific work, and we hope that they will find the essays on materialism helpful. In general, questions of a philosophical character are raised from within very many kinds of intellectual work and practice, and we hope that the majority of these essays will be of use outside the boundaries of academic philosophy departments. Moreover, since in the English-speaking world at least, dominant modes of thought tend to be empiricist and pragmatic in character, we hope that these essays will link up with an alternative theoretical tradition, available to the workers' movement, which already exists in some areas of intellectual work other than philosophy, which speaks in the voices and accents of the cultural environment of that movement, and upon which that movement might draw in its struggle against capital. Hence, here as always, Marxist philosophy is a philosophy which is itself a political practice.

Secondly, it should already be clear from what we have said that the message of these volumes is not a triumphalist one: we do not believe that the authors have produced definitive solutions to the questions they discuss. These are not books of doctrines in search of disciples. Not only are there substantial differences of opinion among the various authors, but there is also in most of the essays a general tentativeness of tone, by and large a sense of modesty about what has been achieved, and an agreement on the need to recognize the fact that Marxist philosophy, in spite of its age, is still very far from having established even the outlines of a settled and confident adult form on many major issues.

John Mepham
David-Hillel Ruben

Introduction to the Third Volume

THIS Third Volume of *Issues in Marxist Philosophy* is devoted to epistemological issues. The central question, as in the previous series, is whether there can be found in Marx's works any specific and important philosophical theory, in this case a theory of knowledge, which can be worked on and elaborated to provide some insight into central philosophical problems. The main subjects of discussion are scientific theories and ideology. The dominant theme of the essays is the radical break which Marx's epistemology makes with other theories of knowledge, and in particular with empiricism and rationalism.

Empiricism, of course, has a long history, and has developed both as philosophical theory and as the implicit methodological basis of most academic social science since Marx's death. In English-speaking countries there has until recently been relatively little native interest in or knowledge of the sciences among philosophers, and this has been especially true in England where academic philosophical training has been concentrated at Oxford, the home of a hegemonic anti-scientific philosophical culture, a university in which the philosophy of science has existed only as a rather marginal and unintegrated specialism. Philosophy of science in England has been represented by the Viennese Popper and the Hungarian Lakatos at the London School of Economics, and in the USA mainly in the work of other emigré European philosophers such as Carnap, Hempel and Nagel. More recently, of course, the rebellious Austrian Paul Feyerabend and the historian Thomas Kuhn have initiated an extremely influential irrationalist and idealist attack on these various imported European empiricisms.

Marxist philosophers have until recently produced no work of significant philosophical merit on epistemological problems. In recent years this situation has slowly begun to change as some Marxists have begun to pay attention to the work of French historians and epistemologists such as Bachelard and Koyré, and to that of the Marxist philosopher most influenced by these writers, Louis Althusser. Althusser's contribution in initiating important work in these fields from a Marxist perspective has been great but equivocal. Without his work most of the essays in this volume would not have been written, and yet they are mostly in disagreement with his work or even hostile to it to one degree or another. More specifically they are hostile to the work of those British Marxist sociologists and economists who have constructed a peculiar version of Althusserian doctrine which, it is argued here, is both idealist and rationalist and which is blind to all that is specifically original and potentially fruitful in Marx's epistemology.

So the main targets of attack here are Anglo-Saxon empiricist social science, the immense and poisonous ideological power of which is emphasized by Roy Edgley, imported European empiricisms and their irrationalist offspring, and the currently influential Marxist alternative on offer from Hindess, Hirst and their disciples. The common aim of the essays is to present and defend a non-empiricist, materialist and realist epistemology.

Andrew Collier and Roy Bhaskar both argue that there can be no *general* 'methodology of science', as has been sought for by empiricism. But this is not because (as the Althusserians would have us believe) thought does not correspond with reality, but because the different sciences have different objects. In general, a materialist theory of science must include (as Althusser's theory does not) an account of the centrality of experiment in science, that is of the fact that the result of an experiment, and thereby the possibility of testing a scientific theory is causally dependent on the nature of the real object and is not the product of thought. Collier, Bhaskar and Sayer all emphasize the fact that the empirical testability of theories does not presuppose (as Feyerabend on the one hand, and Hindess and Hirst on the other, assume) a 'theory-independent language', and nor does it presuppose that scientific knowledge is the product of the confrontation of a passive individual subject with 'the given of experience'. The specificity of the various social sciences, in which experiment is not possible in the way in which it is in the natural sciences, makes the central question for a Marxist epistemology the problem of the relationship between abstract theoretical concepts and 'the concrete analysis of concrete situations' (Lenin).

The authors of these essays also agree on the fact that Marx's epistemology rests on some philosophically acceptable distinction between essence and appearance (a distinction given a systematic exposition in Mepham's article on ideology). This distinction requires an interpretation of 'essence' in terms of causally effective underlying structures (and this is one of the dominant themes of Bhaskar's *Realist Theory of Science*). Such an interpretation does not leave this concept open to common objections against 'essentialism'.

It is argued by Derek Sayer that abstracting the essence from the forms in which reality is experienced is not an empiricist procedure, presupposing a passive observer and his acquaintance with the given of experience; nor is it a method based on an essentialist position, presupposing that concrete, open systems are deducible from the concepts of their essences, or predictable on the basis of knowledge of underlying structures in the same way as is possible for the closed systems constructed in the experimental sciences. This distinction, between open and closed systems, and its epistemological implications, is another central aspect of Bhaskar's account of science. The concrete, being the unity of many determinations, is neither intelligible by passive observation nor reproducible in thought by formalist, deductivist procedures. The concrete is both multiple in its determinations and contradictory in its various underlying essential structures. Hence, as Roy Edgely emphasizes, the necessity for thoroughly non-empiricist procedures, which are both *dialectical* and *critical*.

The problem, however, is not only to give some content to these notions of critical and dialectical thought (and concerning this problem we meet up with the problems which are central to the First Volume of these *Issues in Marxist Philosophy*) but to show how abstraction based on them is a non-arbitrary procedure. In some sense there is method, there are rules or criteria for distinguishing that abstraction which produces scientific theoretical concepts from that which produces theoretical ideology. Arbitrary or superficial abstraction, such as that which is characteristic of empiricist social science, takes concept formation to be simply a matter of mapping empirically observable regularities, and this view is based, as Bhaskar argues, on an unacceptable empiricist idea of causality. Edgley, Sayer and Bhaskar all address themselves to these problems.

Mepham's article on ideology is also based on Marx's distinction between essences and appearances, or phenomenal forms, and on his realist epistemology (and has consequently been attacked by British Althusserians for being 'empiricist'). It also insists on the importance of abstraction and on the fact (which Andrew Collier also emphasizes) that the difference between science and theoretical ideology is an epistemological one (that is they differ in their status as knowledge of reality). The article is weakest in that it claims to be expounding a general theory of ideology. Those epistemological insights in *Capital* on which it is based might be more fruitfully explored in the first instance in relation to a less ambitious problem, namely that of the production specifically of theoretical ideology and the role of critique in the development of a science. The rejoinders to the article by Kathryn Russell and Steve Butters are included here to identify and diagnose these and other weaknesses of Mepham's article.

A shorter version of Andrew Collier's article appeared in *Radical Philosophy* no. 20, 1978. Roy Bhaskar's article originally appeared in the *Journal of Theory of Social Behaviour* VIII, p. 1 (1978), and is reprinted by permission of the publishers, Basil Blackwell. John Mepham's article originally appeared in *Radical Philosophy* no. 2 (1972) and was reprinted together with Steve Butters' 'Response' in *Working Papers in Cultural Studies* no. 6 (1974), and the latter is printed here with the permission of the author and of the editors of that journal.

Marx's Revolutionary Science
ROY EDGLEY

Western Marxism's deviation into philosophy
MARXIST philosophy: how is it possible, and why is it necessary? The union of these two concepts and practices needs explaining and justifying.

Marxism has been a powerful and growing reality for over a century, at first in Europe and more recently in the world as a whole: a reality most obvious at the political level, but within the field of political movements distinguished, among other things, by its unique commitment to theory. Even as theory, however, Marxism presents itself most directly as history, economics, politics, sociology, in a word as science, social science; not as philosophy. Indeed, Marx himself held that 'when reality is depicted, philosophy as an independent branch of knowledge loses its medium of existence' (*The German Ideology*); and in any case, whereas 'the philosophers have only *interpreted* the world in different ways, the point is to *change* it' (*Theses on Feuerbach*, xi). In recalling these words we should not forget that the latter refers to philosophers in the past tense, not philosophy, and that the former, in speaking of philosophy, contains a qualification: 'philosophy *as an independent branch of knowledge*'. Among the absolutely crucial lessons we can learn from Althusser is his comprehensive demonstration that Marxism involves a distinctive philosophy – philosophy not as an independent branch of knowledge but in organic relation with Marxist science and political practice. Marxism is revolutionary root and branch: it opposes the bourgeois *status quo* not only in its political and social practice, and not only in its social scientific theories, but also at the most radical intellectual level of all, the level of philosophy. As a radical *scientific* revolution Marxism contradicts bourgeois theories not simply in their own terms but more basically, replacing their conceptual framework with a new network of categories such

5

as 'mode of production', 'forces of production', 'relations of production', 'surplus-value', etc. More fundamentally, in the process Marxism establishes the specificity of its science at the philosophical level also, founding that science in a radical *philosophical* revolution that reshapes certain more basic concepts. As I shall go on to argue, Althusser fails to appreciate the full depth of this philosophical revolution. But let us note with him for the moment, that Marx's own historical development shows him going through this revolution, signified chiefly in the *Theses on Feuerbach* and *The German Ideology*, as he constructs the basis of his science.

Why is it necessary to discover, articulate, and develop this philosophy? Western Marxism, according to Perry Anderson (*Considerations on Western Marxism*), is a deviation characterized precisely by its preoccupation with philosophy. Since 1920, European Marxism, paradoxically reversing the direction of Marx's own development, has moved towards philosophy in 'the progressive relinquishment of economic or political structures as the central concerns of theory' (p. 49) in 'the classical tradition'. 'Born from the failure of proletarian revolutions in the advanced zones of European capitalism after the First World War, it developed within an ever increasing scission between socialist theory and working-class practice' (p. 92). Becoming more academic, theory became more philosophical, and 'the original relationship between Marxist theory and proletarian practice was subtly but steadily substituted by a new relationship between Marxist theory and bourgeois theory' (p. 55). How then can Marxism need still more philosophy?

It is certainly true that Marxist theory needs more economics and politics, and particularly that it needs to be united with working class practice. Is there then a need for less philosophy? That does not follow. On the contrary, it may be, as Althusser suggests, that the lack of an adequate and explicit Marxist philosophy, articulated from its largely implicit form in Marx's writings and in the process critically developed and militantly disseminated, has left socialism and the working class too exposed to the insidious and often subliminal workings of bourgeois modes of thought, and has thus retarded the growth of Marxist economic and political theory, and with it the real unity of Marxist theory in general with working-class practice. It may be, in other words, that the terrible defeats of the European working class after the Russian Revolution required this agonizingly long detour of Marxism through philosophy – required it because, as Gramsci saw, the advanced bourgeois democracies, especially in the geographical area covered by Western Marxism, maintain their power with the 'spontaneous' consent of the workers ideologically, through hegemony; because this hegemony, working not only through but on intellectuals at the often inexplicit level of philosophy, has inhibited and deformed economic and political theory; and because, as Althusser has argued, even within the socialist movement itself and in Soviet communism in particular, the penetration of bourgeois philosophy has been deep and disastrous: a staggering array of triumphs for bourgeois ideology, and proof of the formidable social power of its philosophy and of the comparative social weakness of the Marxist alternative. This Marxist alternative must grow wherever it can and attack capitalism on all fronts and in all its forms, not as a diversion from the central task of uniting theory with working-class practice but precisely in pursuit of that overriding objective. Anderson's complaint that 'the original relationship between Marxist theory and proletarian practice was subtly but steadily substituted by a new relationship between Marxist theory and bourgeois theory' presents a false antithesis. Marx's theory itself was always in close critical relationship with bourgeois theory, and this very relationship was essential to the programme of undermining the domination of bourgeois thought over the workers (and over intellectuals working in the special fields of economics and politics), and developing the communist class consciousness necessary for the transformation of the Labour movement. Since then, and partly in response to the challenge, to the fear of the spectre that has continued to haunt Europe and beyond, the apparatuses of bourgeois hegemony have grown in power and subtlety, in particular universal education and its complement the media. But their existence as institutional realities, though consolidating the gulf between academic intellectuals and workers, and thus between theory and proletarian practice, at the same time mediates some connection: the students, some of them working class, make contact with intellectuals, and in their turn become teachers whose pupils are working-class children. This is a long way from being enough, and it is certainly necessary for theoreticians and workers to come into much closer relation, in whatever ways possible. But it is significant that though Anderson identifies 'the French Revolt of May 1968' as marking 'a profound historical turning point' in the potential unification of Marxist theory and working-class practice, he entirely omits any reference to the fact that the May revolt had an *academic* centre, that it was led by *university students* as part of a much wider international student movement that started in America, and that there at least a not unimportant role was played by *Western Marxism* in the person of Herbert Marcuse.

In any case, Western Marxism is a Continental pheno-menon, and when one turns from the Continent to the situation over the half-century from 1920 in the English-speaking world, and Britain in particular, one sees a flouri-shing tradition of Marxist work in historical studies but not much Marxism elsewhere. Here, it is not a story of Marxist theory being beaten out of the defeated working class and taking refuge in the universities in the aberrant academic form of philosophy as Western Marxism. The British Labour movement has always been more marked than most in Europe by its lack of theory, the typically British form of bourgeois hegemony, and correspondingly British philosophy has tended to ignore not only politics in general but left-wing politics in particular, remaining impervious to Marxism of any kind, Western or otherwise. The British disease *par excellence* precisely is empiricism, suspicion of theory, and thus a political practice flawed by the petty pragmatism of 'muddling along' and an academic tradition devoid of radical content. Continental universities have intellectuals; we have dons, remote and ineffectual. It is therefore not by any means a case here (or for that matter elsewhere) of continuing where Marx left off, the philosophical revolution gone through and moved beyond, enabling the real business of economics and politics to be tackled. Marxism hardly exists here in any form, and has to be created. Certainly it cannot be found in the official working-class movement, with its trade union consciousness and social democratic politics. But since the student movement of the 60s Marxist theory has begun to take root in British universities and the education system in general, the weakest link of the hegemonic apparatus, and though this is not a growth of theory inside working-class activity it represents an improvement on the previous barren scene and can provide at least one of the conditions hitherto missing for the required unity of theory and proletarian practice: a culture of Marxist theory not across the water and in foreign tongues, but indigenous, in the immediate geographical proximity of the British working class, and therefore, in principle at least, more accessible and available. In particular, the development of Marxist philosophy in the English-speaking world and its continuous struggle against bourgeois ideology can ease the intense and continuous pressure of basic bourgeois forms of thought on English economic, political, and sociological theory, and thus provide more space for the growth of Marxism in those specific areas more directly relevant to the workers' movement.

Theoreticism in science, especially Althusser's
As Anderson points out, Western Marxism, as a type of Marxism in which philosophy preponderates, reveals two major opposed tendencies: first, a Hegelian tendency, exemplified by Lukacs, Korsch, and the Frankfurt school; and more recently, an anti-Hegelian reaction exemplified by Della Volpe, Colletti, and Althusser. Central in this opposition is the question of Marxism as science. Art and culture attract the main interests of the Hegelians, for whom science tends to be a form of bourgeois alienation, whereas the anti-Hegelians attack Hegelian interpretations of Marx chiefly on the ground that Marxist theory is science. I want to show, against both these tendencies, that Marx's science has a philosophical specificity that neither side adequately recognizes, a specificity that can be characterized as Hegelian without reducing its scientificity and materialism. That means exhibiting its structure as dialectical materialism. I will do this by considering Colletti, though only briefly (having criticized his

views in *Critique* VII, Winter 1976/77), and more especially Althusser: both, in my view, cling to conceptions of science that reveal the stubborn power of bourgeois ideology, and in doing so fail to appreciate the real depth of Marx's philosophical revolution, a revolution that reshapes, though in no arbitrary way, the very concepts formed at the centre of bourgeois philosophy in its midwife role during the long birth of modern science, the 'epistemological' concepts of knowledge, rationality, logic and science itself. My argument will show that the detachment of Western Marxism from working-class political practice, though chiefly a practical problem demanding imaginative and adventurous practical strategies, is reflected philosophically in its dominant theory of science. The problem of relating theory to practice is not simply a 'practical' and 'social' problem about how theorists and theory can develop within working-class political activity: it is also a theoretical problem in which the classic bourgeois distinctions between theory and practice need to be theoretically as well as practically attacked and replaced with an understanding of their possible unity that implies a science different not just in its conceptual content but in its very form as theory.

Criticisms of Althusser, his own (*Essays in Self-Criticism*) as well as others' [see for example Norman Geras in *New Left Review*, no. 71 (Jan-Feb 1972), also reprinted in *Western Marxism: A Critical Reader*] have focussed on the 'idealism' or 'theoreticist deviation' in his conception of science: a conception that expresses the general historical development of Western Marxism itself, the detachment of theory from political practice, the practice of the working class. Althusser conceives of science as 'theoretical practice' in distinction from economic, political, and ideological practice, and the general form of the problem is given in his doctrine of the 'relative autonomy' of these distinct practices. What looks favourable under the title of 'autonomy' may seem less desirable as 'independence' and less still when called 'separation' or 'isolation'. Althusser in fact recognizes a historical continuity between ideology and science: a new science establishes itself by working on ideological concepts, but by a revolutionary transformation of this raw material into a new problematic it opens an epistemological break or rupture between itself and its ideological predecessor, a break that involves, in its most general form, a move away from the practical (ideology) towards the less practical (science). According to Althusser, Marxism is such a new science, the science of history. But as he later sees, this account fails to distinguish Marx's science from any other science, and in particular fails to identify the specificity of its unique relation to political practice, especially the political practice of the working class. In his later work, therefore (for example *Essays in Self-Criticism* and *Lenin and Philosophy*), he argues that Marxism breaks not simply with ideology but with bourgeois ideology, so that the break is essentially a political and not simply a theoretical break, achievable only by taking up, as Marx himself did at a crucial phase in his life, a working-class position. This position in political practice can and should be worked out into a theoretical class position represented in a distinctive philosophy, dialectical material- ism. In this way Marxist science is based on Marxist philo- sophy, which is in its turn based on a political position, the position of the working class. This is why 'this science cannot be a science like any other, a science for "everyone". Precisely because it reveals the mechanisms of class exploitation, repression and domination, in the economy, in politics and in ideology, it cannot be recognized by *everyone*' (*Lenin and Philosophy*, p. 7). It is this that constitutes 'the special, unique status which makes Marxist science a *revolutionary* science. Not simply a science which revolutionaries can use in order to make a revolution, but a science which they can use because it rests on *revolutionary class theoretical positions*' (*Essays in Self-Criticism*, p. 130).

Althusser is here, let us remember, trying to correct his 'theoreticist deviation' by conceiving theory in connection with political practice and thus the specificity of Marxist science in its connection with working-class politics. And it has to be said that the new account represents a decisive advance on the old and is full of suggestive and fruitful insights. But it does not go far enough. It constitutes, in fact, an unstable compromise, and when its insights and tenden- cies are developed they will play havoc with much else in

Althusser's 'system'. I want to point out first a curious limitation in his new conception of 'politics in theory': in the field of theoretical practice, shared by science and philosophy, it is philosophy rather than science that takes on the burden of politics. The change in his position is summarized chiefly in the theme that runs so insistently through his later work, 'that philosophy is fundamentally *political*' (*Lenin and Philosophy*, p. 15), that 'Philosophy is politics in the field of theory' (*Essays in Self-Criticism*, p. 68), that 'the intervention of *class theoretical positions*' is 'what could be called the intervention of the philosophical "instance"' (*Essays in Self-Criticism*, p. 149). 'In theoretically overestimating philosophy', he writes (*Essays in Self-Criticism*, p. 150), 'I underestimated it *politically*'. It is in accordance with this changed doctrine that Althusser characterizes philosophy no longer as the 'Theory of theoretical practice' but instead as 'class struggle in the field of theory'. What is more, significantly, this new characterization distinguishes philosophy from science. His reference (*Essays in Self-Criticism*, p. 142) to 'philosophy, which is not (a) science, but class struggle in theory' clearly implies, what is implicit throughout, that science, even Marxist science, is *not* class struggle in theory. The thesis that 'philosophy is politics in the field of theory', which in more general terms is the thesis of 'the *primacy of the practical function over the theoretical function* in philosophy itself' (*Essays in Self-Criticism*, p. 143), thus protects the peculiarly theoretical status of science itself. Marxist science is not class struggle in theory, not itself politics in the field of theory, because it is, so to speak, not 'practical' enough: because it is still theory; because it is still theory, I shall argue, in the sense in which, in Althusser's view, all good science, Marxist and otherwise, is theory. His 'theoreticism' survives here, and with it, as I will show, his failure to appreciate the full depth of Marx's philosophical revolution, the full specificity of Marx's science, and in particular, the full, indeed the most crucial, sense of the revolutionary nature of that science.

Science vs ideology : in what does the theoretical status of science consist ?

Why, in theorizing the relation between Marxist science and

proletarian political practice, does Althusser insist on shifting the political burden onto philosophy in order to retain the theoretical status of science? And in what exactly does that theoretical status consist? The answer to these questions lies surely with his conception of ideology and its distinction from science; though this answer also raises the further questions of the distinction between philosophy and ideology, and of how, Marxist science having been based on philosophy, communism can then produce 'an ideology which will depend on a science ... ' (*Reading Capital*, p. 131). Whatever the answers to these questions, Althusser's immediate problem is to understand the connection between Marxist science and working-class politics while maintaining the distinction between that science and ideology. For 'ideology, as a system of representations, is distinguished from science in that in it the practico-social function is more important than the theoretical function (function as knowledge)' ('Marxism and Humanism' in *For Marx*, p. 231). In his glossary, authorized by Althusser, Ben Brewster slips into this characterization of ideology the claim that ideology 'is distinguished from a science not by its falsity, for it can be coherent and logical (for instance, theology)'; but this is disingenuous in the face of the many passages, identified by Geras, in which Althusser associates ideology with 'a realm of mystification and deformation, of illusion, falsehood and myth, of confusion, prejudice and arbitrariness, of the imaginary and non-knowledge' (*Western Marxism: A Critical Reader*, p. 271). Certainly, though an ideology can be 'theoretical' (for example, *For Marx*, p. 13) and 'a system of representations' (see the quote above) it is not knowledge, despite the fact that it is commonly taken to be knowledge: as theory, one might say, ideology is defective, and it is in this respect that science on Althusser's view, when it establishes itself by a rupture with ideology, represents an advance.

Is it the case, then, that ideology fails as theory, fails to be knowledge, *because* of its predominantly 'practico-social function'? Ideology 'presupposes both a real relation and an *"imaginary"*, *"lived"* relation ... In ideology the real relation is inevitably invested in the imaginary relation, a relation that *expresses* a *will* (conservative, conformist, reformist or revolutionary), a hope or a nostalgia, rather than describing a reality' (*For Marx*, pp. 233–4). Shortly after this passage, Althusser resumes his case against humanism as an ideological rather than a scientific concept by repeating this point about the connection between ideology and will, and then goes on to relate this to the presence of a 'value judgement' in humanism:

> 'When, in the relations between Marxists and everyone else, the former lay stress on a socialist personal humanism, they are simply demonstrating their *will* to bridge the gap that separates them from possible allies ... Speaking of the idea of man and humanism in *The German Ideology*, Marx commented that the idea of human nature, or of the essence of man, concealed a *coupled value judgement*, to be precise, the couple human/inhuman' (*For Marx*, pp. 236–7).

In elaborating on 'the two realities' of theory and class struggle (*Lenin and Philosophy*, p. 23) Althusser distinguishes theory as what 'enables us to understand the laws of history', and a similar presupposition about the nature of theory lies behind what he objects to in humanism (*Essays in Self-Criticism*, p. 20): 'the *theoretical* pretensions of the humanist conception to explain society and history'. As these quotations show, science for Althusser is centrally a matter of laws and explanation: and one thing that this conception of scientific theory rules out is identified on p.187, where he refers to Marxism's need to 'grasp, in the strong sense, the "obvious" truth that the revolutions which we know are either premature or miscarried, but from within a theory which dispenses with the normative notions of prematurity and of miscarriage, that is, with a normative standpoint ... '.

The conclusion seems irresistible that what has been at work from the beginning in Althusser's conception of science and its distinction from ideology, and what continues to survive the rigours of his self-criticism, is a very familiar article of bourgeois philosophy: science as knowledge because it is descriptive and thus as theory value-free and in that sense theoretical, ideology as cognitive illusion because it is evaluative, prescriptive, and practical. This would explain his objection to the thesis of an 'end of ideology' (*For Marx*, p. 232). He disagrees with Daniel Bell on the social need for ideology, but shares with him this basic part of the conceptual distinction between ideology and science.

How then can Althusser think Marxist science as theoretical and not political in this sense while at the same time acknowledging its political basis? What precisely is the nature of this relation in which science is said to be 'based on' a political position? How can a political position be the basis for a science that is not itself 'politics in theory'? In consistency, Althusser must conceive of the political position, perhaps metaphorically, as a *vantage point* from which the real nature of the social structure, otherwise hidden, becomes visible; or if that is too 'empiricist' a way of putting it, he must suppose that the knowledge constituted by Marxist science cannot be produced or recognized as knowledge except from the class political position of the proletariat. From any other 'point of view' (including, if that is possible, a point of view that is not a class or political point of view at all?), this knowledge, despite its apolitical character as (pure?) theory, must remain hidden; in any other position, the efforts of theoretical practice to produce a theoretical knowledge of history will inevitably prove barren. This does in fact seem to be the implication of the passage already quoted from *Lenin and Philosophy*, p. 7: 'this science cannot be a science like any other, a science for "everyone". Precisely because it reveals the mechanisms of class exploitation, repression and domination . . . it cannot be recognized by *everyone*'. This passage of course raises the question, raised by Geras (*Western Marxism: A Critical Reader*, pp. 270–1), of how the presence of such concepts as exploitation, repression, and domination is compatible with 'a theory which dispenses with . . . a normative standpoint'; but presumably Althusser thinks of the theory itself as explanatory and thus as focusing less on the exploitation than on 'the mechanisms' behind it. At any rate, his point is that this science cannot be 'recognized' except from a working-class political position, and a similar point is made elsewhere: 'This political position must be worked out into a theoretical (philosophical) position so that the causes and mechanisms of what is visible from the proletarian standpoint may be grasped and understood' (*Essays in Self-Criticism*, p. 161); and 'it is only from the point of view of the exploited class that it is possible to discover . . . the mechanisms of those relations of exploitation, the relations of production of a class society' (*Lenin and Philosophy*, p. 8). The political position is here depicted as a necessary condition for the production and recognition of the scientific theory, but as *external* to that theory's content.

But the relation between Marxist theory and working-class practice is not just a one-way but (at least) a two-way relation: it is a question not only of how such a theory can be 'based on' that practice but also of how that practice can be 'based on' such a theory. Althusser frequently refers to this direction of the relation, and often by means of this opaque relational term 'based on' (*For Marx*, pp. 167, 175, 176). But sometimes he is more explicit. Marxist science is 'a science which revolutionaries can use in order to make a revolution', and 'a weapon in their revolutionary class struggle' (*Essays in Self-Criticism*, pp.130 and 152). More explicitly still, 'Marxists know that there can be no tactics that do not depend on a strategy – and no strategy that does not depend on theory' (*For Marx*, p. 241). Most explicitly of all, and here again asserting, but this time with explicit emphasis, the exteriority of the relation, 'Theoretical practice produces knowledges which can then figure as *means* that will serve the ends of a technical practice . . . the relation between technique and knowledge is an *external*, unreflected relation . . . It is this exteriority which justifies Lenin's thesis of the necessity to *import* Marxist theory into the spontaneous political practice of the working class' (*For Marx*, p. 171, 7n). What Althusser is objecting to here as 'the most dangerous ideological menace' is 'the creation and success of so-called theories which have nothing to do with real theory but are mere *by-products* of technical activity'. What he is not objecting to is the use of 'real theory' as a means in technical practice, that is as providing a technology, a guide to strategy. Indeed, given his value-free 'theoreticist' conception of science, this is the only practical function thinkable for theory: theory as explanation, as description of 'mechanisms', has a bearing on practice by revealing what effects actions will have and thus what can be achieved and by what means. As Hume long ago saw, for such a science to have this practical bearing, aims and interests must be presupposed, and if this science is to criticize some working-class aims, as Althusser says, it can do so only if others are given, given independently and from outside the critical scope of that science. For Marxist science on Althusser's interpretation, the exteriority that justifies Lenin's thesis is at this level the exteriority of ultimate working-class interests, for the fulfilment of which Marxist science provides a strategy, the strategy of revolution. This is the exteriority in general of science to politics, not the specific unity of Marxist theory and working-class practice. Scientific socialism, on this view, becomes what it has so often been before, a conjunction not a unification of science and political action, a conjunction in which the science, being 'theory', needs to be supplemented by something else that will mediate its connection with practice, an ethics or an ideology. The Second International exacts its 'posthumous revenge' in subtle and paradoxical ways: here its spirit, no mere ghost surviving the death and burial of that body but incarnate as always in the bourgeois ideology of science, Enlightenment rationalism, possesses the exorcist himself.

From scientific values to dialectic

Geras protests that in his discussion of *Capital*, Althusser is 'wrong to pretend that it contains no values of any kind whatever' (*Western Marxism: A Critical Reader*, p. 271). But he devotes no more than a paragraph to the point; and his references to the 'ethical and critical content' of Marx's concept of exploitation and to Marx's use of this concept as 'a critical as well as a cognitive one' do not explain how these values might be other than ethical, and they are in any case compatible with a relation between cognitive and critical content that is purely conjunctive and thus not necessarily, contrary to what he suggests, an alternative to Hilferding.

What needs to be grasped is how Marx's theory involves values, employs evaluative concepts, without at those points ceasing to be science and becoming ethical or ideological. And in this task one of the words Geras uses is absolutely crucial: the word 'critical'. To criticize something is to appraise or evaluate it, usually negatively, that is to object to it, reject it, to oppose or attack it, generally in words, and thus in those words to call for it to be changed; and this concept echoes and re-echoes throughout Marx's work, from first to last, often in association with the word 'revolutionary' (for example, (*Theses on Feuerbach*, 1).

It is evident that criticism is not necessarily ethical or ideological or otherwise non-scientific. On the contrary, science must, as science, involve criticism: this critical function is not something external to and merely conjoined with its cognitive function; each is logically dependent on the other. Any theory, as theory, stands (explicitly or by implication) in critical relation with other (actual or possible) theories: namely, with those that it contradicts. What Althusser calls 'theoretical practice' or 'theoretical production' is also theoretical destruction, an activity in which scientists criticize existing theories and concepts and in the process transform that 'raw material' into a more adequate theoretical product.

So much is hardly contestable, though the common doctrine that science is value-free at least obscures the matter. It does so because it focuses, like the traditional bourgeois epistemology of which it forms a part, on the truth-relation of theory, that is on the relation between theory and its object, the relation between theory and the reality that theory is true (or false) of. The doctrine that science is descriptive and not evaluative or prescriptive can then be seen as a characterization of that relation between theory and its object; and this is compatible with an evaluative and critical relation between theory and theory. Acceptable for natural science, and embodied in the bourgeois philosophy of science that takes natural science as instantiating the timeless essence of science in general, this is one central aspect of the ideology that Marx, labouring to make a specifically *social* science in the self-knowledge of its specificity, begins explicitly to break with in the *Theses on Feuerbach*. The social science he accordingly creates is revolutionary in more than one sense: not only in the sense explicated by Bachelard or Kuhn, a sense in which Galilean science is revolutionary, by radically breaking with and overthrowing existing theory and its conceptual framework; not only in the sense in which political revolutionaries can use it as technology for strategic guidance; Marx's science is revolutionary in both of these ways chiefly because its relation not only to other theories but also to its object is critical, and therefore requires *from its own scientific standpoint* the revolutionary transformation both of other theories and of their common object, society itself.

How is this possible? It is this possibility that is provided for by the dialectic, the dialectic in Marx's 'rational form', the materialist dialectic. The word is not used in the *Theses on Feuerbach*, but the concept is implicit in its dominating theme, the rejection of traditional Enlightenment materialism with its 'theoretical stance', its standpoint of 'observation', 'contemplation', 'interpretation', and Marx's alternative of ' "revolutionary", . . . "practical-critical" activity'. When, nearly three decades later, Marx in a famous passage in a preface to *Capital* declares that his scientific method is 'a scandal and abomination to bourgeoisdom and its doctrinaire professors . . . because it lets nothing impose upon it, and is in its essence critical and revolutionary', he explicitly associates this 'critical and revolutionary' character of his science with his form of the dialectic. Dialectical materialism rejects traditional materialism because traditional materialism knows nothing of dialectic and consequently conceives the relation between theory and object as non-critical, as descriptive and interpretative. Dialectical materialism rejects the Hegelian dialectic because of its idealism, which knows nothing of real material practice. In the logical unification of theory and practice achieved by the materialist dialectic the practical revolutionary transformation of society is reflected in and guided by a theory that is *critical of that society*.

The key to the understanding of this unity, and specifically to the critical nature of Marx's science, is contained in the phrase immediately following the passage just quoted about the dialectic: 'The contradictions inherent in the movement of capitalist society . . . '. This category of contradiction, this time in explicit relation with the unity of critical theory and revolutionary practice, makes its appearance also in Marx's *Theses on Feuerbach*. Speaking of Feuerbach's materialist understanding of religion, which 'consists in resolving the religious world into its secular basis', Marx contrasts this with the emerging dialectical character of his own materialism:

> that the secular basis lifts off from itself and establishes itself as an independent realm in the clouds can only be explained in terms of the inwardly riven and inwardly contradictory character of this secular basis. This itself must therefore both be understood in its contradiction and revolutionized in practice. Therefore once for example the earthly family is revealed as the secret of the holy family, the former must then itself be destroyed in theory and in practice (*Theses on Feuerbach* iv).

What Marx is in effect asserting here, as a cardinal doctrine of the materialist dialectic, is the doctrine of contradictions in reality; and this is a presupposition of what makes it 'a scandal and abomination to bourgeoisdom and its doctrinaire professors', its 'critical and revolutionary' character, because the concept of contradiction is essentially a critical concept, a category of scientific criticism. A familiar judgement of Althusser's work is that though it is flawed by his idealist or theoreticist conception of science, his understanding of contradiction and dialectic in the essays 'Contradiction and Overdetermination' and 'On the Materialist Dialectic' (*For Marx*) is free of these flaws and of more lasting value. I want to suggest that his theoreticist conception of science rests on inadequacies in his accounts of contradiction and dialectic.

These inadequacies are constituted by an omission, by a silence, as Althusser himself might say. That silence announces itself when one conceives of the tradition of Western Marxism as divided about the axis of Hegel, with the anti-Hegelian movement most powerfully represented by Althusser and the school of della Volpe, especially Colletti. For in this alliance, Colletti's anti-Hegelianism includes Althusser as an opponent. Althusser accepts the doctrine of contradictions in reality, dialectical materialism, and even a dialectics of nature (*Lenin and Philosophy*, p. 117). Colletti rejects them all. His anti-Hegelianism takes the form of the claim that science and materialism are incompatible with the Hegelian principle that there are contradictions in reality: since contradiction, as a specifically logical relation distinct from that of conflict, can exist only in thought or theory, as a relation between propositions, there can be no contradictions in the reality that is the material object of thought or theory; as Kant saw, real opposition is not logical opposition; that there are contradictions in reality is thus a specifically idealist doctrine; and dialectical materialism must therefore be abandoned. But the fact is that Althusser is only doubtfully comprehended within Colletti's criticism; for he does not so much deny these theses as not even raise the questions to which they are answers, and in consequence his version of dialectical materialism is hardly recognizable as such in Colletti's terms. His materialist transformation of Hegel's dialectic is chiefly concerned to argue that real contradiction is not, as in Hegel, simple, 'or more exactly contradiction in the logical sense of the term, whose terms are two equal entities each simply bearing one of the contrary signs + or −, A or not-A' (*Essays in Self-Criticism*, p.184): it is, rather, complex, uneven, and overdetermined, as when 'two quite unequal classes confront each other', though this confrontation 'certainly is a contradiction since the *relation of confrontation reproduces the conditions of confrontation* instead of transcending them in a beautiful Hegelian exaltation and reconciliation' (p.185). This simply fails to consider the way in which Colletti's argument renders dialectical materialism problematic. For Colletti, the crucial distinction for a proposed materialist transformation of Hegel's dialectic is the distinction between thought and reality, not between the simple and the complex. What Althusser calls 'contradiction in the logical sense of the term' might 'more exactly' be identified as contradiction in the sense given to it in the formalization of logic, that is in the special discipline of formal logic. Even here this 'simple' and 'even' relation between a proposition and its negation can occur within a much more complex and uneven context – but still a context of propositions, or at least propositional forms. Outside such formalization, in thought and theory with a content, the relation of contradiction is still more complex, even and overdetermined, as in the relation between Galilean and Aristotelian dynamics, for instance – but again, Colletti could argue, it remains a relation between propositions, contents of thought. When Althusser refers to class confrontation as 'certainly . . . a contradiction, since the *relation of confrontation reproduces the conditions of confrontation*' this may be an advance on the totally unspecific and unilluminating characterization of contradiction in the glossary of *For Marx* ('a term for the articulation of a practice into the complex whole of the social formation'), but without further explanation it must appear arbitrary, as if 'contradiction in the logical sense' and 'contradiction' in this sense were mere homonyms.

Where epistemological materialism fails: social science as 'critique'

But why should Althusser's ignoring of Colletti's questions be considered an omission, a failure, a silence in which there is something to say, a gap of unspoken words? For a start, they are not just Colletti's questions. Colletti here represents a substantial historical reality: a reality in which, in my view, bourgeois ideology speaks loud and clear, even, as in this case again, from within the Marxist tradition. That ideology is precisely the dominant bourgeois epistemology of science constituted by Enlightenment materialism and castigated by Marx in the *Theses on Feuerbach* – castigated for being, to use the word that is absent though its concept is present, undialectical. Colletti tends to use the word 'dialectical' for 'logical opposition', that is for any contradiction, as if the mere recognition of contradiction in thought, for example by logical positivism or Popper's falsificationism, were sufficient to make these theories dialectical. Althusser, on the other hand, seems to think that a theory of nature is dialectical as long as it recognizes that nature is a process without a subject (*Lenin and Philosophy*, pp. 117–19); which makes it difficult to distinguish between dialectical and a thoroughgoing mechanical materialism. These undialectical conceptions of dialectic within Western Marxism, and the general survival of Enlightenment materialism, reflect the twin pressures of working-class defeat and the success of bourgeois technology and natural science, and more specifically at the theoretical level the academic rebirth of formal logic through Frege and Russell, with its self-reflective philosophy of logic echoing unmistakably in the work of Althusser and the school of della Volpe. Not only is it the case that Colletti's questions about dialectical materialism are not simply Colletti's questions, they are questions for which at least their space is left within Althusser's own work itself. The specific location of this space is the epistemological materialism that Althusser shares with Colletti, in particular its irreducible distinction between reality and thought and the primacy of the former over the latter. Althusser marks this distinction in many ways, for example in his distinction between the real object and the object of knowledge, in Marx's distinction between the historical order of the development of society and the order of thought about it, in Spinoza's distinction between the dog that barks and the concept of the dog that does not. He nowhere considers the way that Colletti marks it, the way in which the epistemological materialism dominant in bourgeois ideology marks it, and which at least, therefore, needs to be confronted: by identifying thought and theory as the locus of logical relations such as contradiction, and distinguishing these from the chronological, spatial, causal, and social relations that structure reality.

From the point of view of a materialism that sees Hegel as its chief threat and target, the irreducible distinction between reality and thought presents itself as an irreducibility with a definite direction: 'the materialist thesis of the irreducibility of being to thought' (*Considerations on Western Marxism*, p. 63). But is this to fall into the dualistic arms of Descartes or Kant? What has happened to the materialist thesis of the reducibility of thought to reality? One may accept Althusser's valuable point, that Marx's materialism is not a monism in the traditional sense, a doctrine about substance. Marx's materialism is social materialism, in which the classical problem of the relation between thought and matter is replaced by the problem of the relation between theory and practice. Nor is Marx's materialism reductionist. But at the minimum it recognizes the practical, social, and historical reality of thought and theory. In particular, it recognizes thought and theory as part of the real object of social science, part of the social reality that this science must theorize in its structural unity.

In other words, the simple duality of relations in which a natural scientific theory stands, on the one hand its descriptive and non-evaluative relation to its real object, and on the other its evaluative and critical relation to other theories, must break down for any adequate science of society. Thought and theory, in particular about society, including existing scientific theories with which it competes, including even itself, must be part of that real social object that social science seeks to understand and theorize. It must as science stand in critical relation to competing theories and ideas, which it contradicts. But it cannot, like natural science, leave them simply repudiated, as errors, illusions, mistakes, or slips, otherwise unexplained. It must understand these thoughts and theories as part of its real object, and for scientific materialism that means comprehending them in structural unity with their social basis in material practice. It is at this point, taking thought as its real object, that a Marxism in thrall to epistemological materialism opens the way for the self-refuting relativism of the sociology of knowledge, forgetting its own status as science and thus its critical relation to other thought. What Marxism on the contrary does is not merely to insist on the theoretical defects of its opponent theories, and then trace them causally to aspects of the material social structure, as if these aspects were otherwise neutral and innocent. More strongly, it imputes those theoretical defects to aspects of the material social structure that are themselves defective, in particular to contradictions in that structure. This is what Marx calls 'critique', and *Capital* is a monumental example of it: criticism of the theories of political economy that is at the same time a critical analysis of the capitalist mode of production itself.

Colletti and other materialists who reject the doctrine of contradictions in reality do so because of their obsessive preoccupation with the central concern of traditional epistemology, the truth-relation of theory, that is, the relation of theory to its real object. In insisting on the independence of the real object from theory, and thus on its distinctiveness in relation to theory, they at the same time commit themselves to the distinctiveness of theory in relation to the real object. It is in this way that materialism as an epistemological doctrine so often turns out to be a dualism, in which a materialism of the real object is combined with an idealism of theory and thought. Given this structure of ideas, the question whether there are contradictions in reality presents itself as the question whether, given that contradiction is a logical relation and thus a relation between the propositional contents of thought, a contradictory proposition is ever *true of* reality. Colletti is right to argue that science could not embrace such nonsense. But he fails to see the significance of a different interpretation of the question. Since thought and theory are also part of reality and thus real objects that can be thought about, contradictions in thought, though not *true of* reality, certainly *exist in* reality; and it is only because they do *exist in* reality that they can be the object of criticism—

criticism for failing to be *true of* reality. Moreover, it is because two contradictory theories cannot both be true that each bears a critical relation to the other: instantiated in actual thought this relation of logical opposition is in fact a critical relation of real opposition, Kant notwithstanding. It is no less logical opposition and no more simply natural 'conflict of forces' for taking the form of real social and historical struggle.

Given all this, Marx's extension of the logical concept of contradiction from its site in theory to social practice in general, though it reshapes the concept, is anything but arbitrary. If Kant is to be brought into the dispute, one should remember that the concept of logic connects not only with that of logos, words, but also with that of reason, and that Kant thought that reason could be not only theoretical but also practical. A materialist social science that retains, as it must as science, its commitment to logic, and in particular to the logical criticism and contradiction of its predecessor theories, while at the same time, in its specificity as *social* science, comprehending the thought of society, including itself and its predecessor theories, as part of its real object, and materialistically, in structural relation with social practice in general, requires this conceptual revolution in which it discovers the critical isomorphism between the structure of society's thought and the structure of its material life: the critical isomorphism identified in the category of real contradiction, a category basic to and presupposed by all the other critical concepts that Marx's science generates.

Though a system of thought that is contradictory cannot be true *of* its real object, this isomorphic relation between the structure of a society's thought and the structure of its material life thus gives sense to the idea that such thought is true *to* that material life: in being contradictory it 'reflects' and so discloses, though its content does not explicitly assert, the contradictory structure of the material life of that society. It is this that accounts for the peculiarity of Marx's method pointed out by Colletti (for example in 'Marxism: Science or Revolution?' in *Ideology in Social Science*, R. Blackburn (ed), p. 373): a method that leads to the criticism of a theory on the ground of its truth – in this sense.

This materialist conception of logic signified by the dialectical category of real contradiction not only provides for the crucial innovation of a science that is critical of its object: it does so without in the least diverting that science from its explanatory role. More strongly, in this science criticism and explanation are not simply conjoined, but unified in this very category of real *logical* opposition, in the conception of a social structure in which conflict, antagonism, and struggle are the motors of historical change. Under this unification, moreover, this process of change is not simply *predicted*, in the manner of natural science: just as Marx revolutionizes the bourgeois category of value-neutral explanation by making explanation, or what he sometimes calls analysis, critical, so in the same conversion he takes that other chief pillar of bourgeois science, prediction, and unifies it with the practical category of *intention*, the proletariat's intention, articulated and rationally justified in Marx's science, to change the world of capitalism by revolution into socialism.

Althusser rightly speaks of Marx's 'immense theoretical revolution'. I have argued that the continuing theoreticist tendency in his understanding of Marxist science is a bourgeois survival, a survival due to his failure to appreciate the full philosophical depth of Marx's *theoretical* revolution and thus the way in which Marxist science, without deserting its scientific standpoint, constitutes itself theoretically as the mouthpiece of the workers' movement and their *political* revolution. The full specificity, that is distinctiveness, of Marxist science is marked not simply by the specificity of its *specific* concepts, such as mode of production and relations of production, but also by the specificity of its more *generic* concepts, such as those of science, knowledge, and reason. The most explicit of these transformed generic concepts is that of contradiction, and one should not omit to number it among the rest: especially when the chief concern, in considering Marx's science, is 'the question of its *relation to its object*, hence both the question of the specificity of its *object*, and the question of the specificity of its *relation* to that object' (*Reading Capital*, p.14). I mean, of course, the relation of Marx's science to its *real* object, what it aims at in theory and practice: the social structure and its revolutionary transformation.

Science as Critique:
Marx vs Althusser*

DEREK SAYER

I

ALTHUSSER's *Reading Capital* probably did more to open up current debates over Marx's epistemology than any other single work. If its authors have since retreated from their 1966 stance, their epigones, especially in Britain, have not.[1] This paper is about Marx, not his interpreters. But its conclusions directly challenge the reading of Marx associated with Althusser, and the challenge is basic enough to be worth making explicit. I will therefore begin by rehearsing some of the Althusserians' central claims.

Althusser starts *Reading Capital* pt. 1 (1966) with a discourse on epistemology (see Hindess and Hirst, *Pre-Capitalist Modes of Production*, Introduction) and seeks to ground historical materialism in a specifically epistemological break with the problematic he sees as common to both empiricism and idealism. This problematic, he alleges, identifies the object of knowledge with the real object of which it is the knowledge. Science is thus conceived as a process of extraction (abstraction) of the 'essential' from the 'inessential' real, and the problem of knowledge is accordingly seen as one of guaranteeing the correspondence of concepts to reality.

Against this, Althusser imputes to Marx a rigorous distinction between the real and the object of knowledge, and a conception of science as a process of production 'which takes place entirely within thought' (*Reading Capital*, 56; see *Pre-Capitalist Models of Production*, p. 3). He elaborates the latter via his '3 Generalities' schema. Scientific knowledge (G3) is not extracted from the real but produced by the action

* I would like to thank John Jervis and John Mepham for their comments on my previous work on various of the issues treated in this paper.

of the concepts of a scientific problematic (G2) on existing
more or less ideological notions (G1).[2] Between G1 and G3
there is no identity of essence but a transformation. Metaphors of extraction and essence/appearance distinctions are
therefore misleading, and must be rejected. So too must
be the classical problem of knowledge, for in this
schema thought and reality never confront one another
directly.

This has clear implications for the nature of scientific
concepts. In the idealist/empiricist problematic, so Althusserians hold, concepts are regarded as descriptive of, and
therefore constructed by abstraction from and validated
by reference to the real. This is no longer the case
in the problematic they ascribe to Marx. Here, the concepts
(G3) which embody knowledge are constructed by the
transformation of other concepts (G1) and validated by
their conformity not to the real, but to theoretical criteria
'one hundred per cent internal' to the problematic whose
product they are (*Reading Capital*, p. 59; see *Pre-Capitalist
Modes of Production*, pp. 1–5, 320–3). And the concepts of
the theory which plays the determinate role in Althusser's
scheme (G2) are *a priori* constructs, and not in any sense
descriptions but 'means for the analysis of' the empirical and
concrete (*Pre-Capitalist Modes of Production*, p. 4).[3] Interest-
ingly (for the merely formal Generalities model does not
oblige it) Althusserians normally subsume most of Marx's
major concepts under this G2 rubric. Hindess and Hirst, for
instance, include amongst their 'means for the production of
knowledge' 'the concepts of the various modes of production
and of their conditions of existence' (*ibid*). It is tempting to
cut through the finer points of debate and remark that it is
hardly surprising that they find no room for history in their
Marxism.

It is also tempting to dwell on the problems to which this
position gives rise; to wonder, perhaps, at how Althusser can
consistently maintain that 'the real object . . . is the absolute
reference point for the knowledge that is concerned with it'
(*Reading Capital*, p. 156) or at how a radically conventionalist epistemology[4] is able to sustain a universal science/ideo-
logy distinction. But my concern here is with Marx, and

these are not, in my view, Marx's problems. For Marx, I hope to show, was in Althusser's terms an empiricist *par excellence*.

II

Althusser is of course correct in his assertion that Marx distinguished the real from knowledge of the real. He omits to mention that in Marx this is a prosaically commonsensical distinction made in a specific context: against Hegel's speculative habit of making the concept the demiurge of reality.[5] Althusser is also right, in a backhanded sort of fashion, in his contention that for Marx the correspondence of concepts and reality was not an issue. But this was not because Marx repudiated the problem. It was because he aggressively espoused one particular solution to it – the materialist solution, which consists at root in assuming precisely this correspondence.

This should hardly require demonstration, but a reminder of the real Marx will not be untimely: 'neither thoughts nor language ... form a world of their own ... they are only *manifestations* of actual life' (*The German Ideology*, p. 504), 'men, who produce their social relations in accordance with their material productivity, also produce ideas, categories, that is to say the abstract ideal expression of these same social relations' (Letter to Annenkov, 1846 in *The Poverty of Philosophy*, p. 189). These passages are from writings Althusser classifies as 'works of the break', one of whose major themes is that ideas are but 'the independent expression in thought of the existing world', language 'the language of reality' (*The German Ideology*, pp. 102, 57). But the theme is not transitory; it is restated, forcefully and at length, as late as 1880 (in a text that has received the ultimate Althusserian accolade of translation in *Theoretical Practice*).[6] Marx argues, against Adolf Wagner,

> in no sense do men begin by 'standing in this theoretical relation to *things of the external world*'. They begin like every animal, by eating, drinking, etc., that is not by 'standing' in a relation but by *actively responding*, by mastering certain things of the external world by deeds and thus satisfying their needs. (That is, they begin with

production.) [...] At a certain level of development ... they reach
the stage of linguistic baptism for the whole class of these things
distinguished from the rest of the external World experientially.
[...] But this linguistic designation simply expresses as an image
what repeated confirmation has made an experience ... (Notes on
Adolf Wagner, p. 46).

It might be noted finally that the very text which forms the
launching point for Althusser's epistemological peregrina-
tions, Marx's General Introduction of 1857, itself reiterates
that categories 'express ... the forms of being, the characteristics of existence' and moreover emphasizes that 'this holds
for science as well' (*Grundrisse*, p. 106).

I cite these passages, however, less to contradict Althusser
than to introduce an issue which bears centrally on Marx's
conception of science. This concerns ideology. The latter
concept, which may roughly be defined as connoting a body
of ideas characterized by its overall falsity, is a key one in
Marx's discourse. Recent literature[7] has rightly tended to
stress that for Marx ideology is not reducible to an error of
perception (including an error induced by propaganda) on the
part of its victim but arises rather from an accurate perception of how things 'represent themselves' (*Capital*, I, p. 537)
to experience. In Godelier's words 'it is not the subject who
deceives himself, but *reality* which deceives him' (*Ideology
in Social Science*, R. Blackburn, (ed.) p. 337). The mystificatory mechanism, in other words, is an objective one, analogous
to that which produces a mirage.

I shall not labour this point, for it has been well explicated,
and more than adequately documented, elsewhere. I wish
instead to make just one simple, and to my mind neglected
observation. It is that in view of his general theses on consciousness (like those quoted above) Marx could not consistently have explained ideology otherwise. Those theses posit
a relation of correspondence between categories of thought
and forms of experience (*phenomenal forms*, in Marx's par-
lance). To construe ideology as arising out of the subject's
errors of perception would be to deny precisely this correspondence, and affirm once more the independence of consciousness from experience. This option is therefore closed
to Marx. He must accept that experience itself is the principal

'means of ideological production'. This in turn implies that an explanation of ideology must take the form of an excavation of those mechanisms, within the real, which are responsible for its deceptive self-presentation. In fine, and *pace* Althusser, Marx must employ an appearance/essence distinction. It is the only way he can reconcile his assertion of the falsity of ideology with his materialist theory of consciousness. Marx himself, I might stress, explicitly sees his science in these terms:

> the philistines' and vulgar economists' *way of looking at things* stems from . . . the fact that it is only the direct *form of manifestation* of relations that is reflected in their brains and not their *inner connection*. Incidentally, if the latter were the case what need would there be of *science*? (Letter to Engels, 27 June 1867, *Selected Correspondence*).

> all science would be superfluous if the outward appearance and the essence of things directly coincided (*Capital*, III, p. 817).

III

Thus far I have sought to question the Althusserian depiction of the epistemological basis for Marx's notion of science. But one might still perhaps be tempted to accept the '3 Generalities' model as an acceptable account of Marx's procedures for constructing scientific concepts. Some more specific observations are therefore called for.

First, it is necessary to emphasize that Marx repeatedly characterized his own methodology as empirical. *The German Ideology* expresses this in prescriptive as well as descriptive terms;

> The premises from which we begin are not arbitrary ones, not dogmas, but real premises from which abstraction can only be made in the imagination. They are the real individuals, their activity, and the material conditions under which they live . . . These premises can thus be verified in a purely empirical way (*The German Ideology*, p. 31).

> Empirical observation must in each separate instance bring out

empirically, and without any mystification and speculation, the
connection of the social and political structure with production.
(*ibid*, p. 36, see also pp. 38, 40).

Lest, once again, this be dismissed as the positivism of Marx's
immaturity, let me for a second time quote his 1880 Notes on
Wagner. Note that in this case Marx is talking specifically
about concept formation, which he sees as an emphatically
a posteriori activity, and that his object is to clarify, against
Wagner's misreading, what he actually did in *Capital*. He
writes,

> De prime abord I do not start from 'concepts' . . . What I start from
> is the simplest social form in which the labour product is represented
> in contemporary society, and this is the '*commodity*'. I analyze this,
> and, indeed, first in *the form in which it appears* [. . .] Thus it is not
> I who divide 'value' into use-value and exchange-value as oppositions
> into which the abstraction 'value' divides itself, but the *concrete
> social form* of the labour product. (Notes on Adolf Wagner, pp. 50,
> 51; see also pp. 45, 52).

Such 'empiricism', in short, is a consistent motif which per-
vades Marx's work.

There is, however, an apparent exception; the account of
'obviously the scientifically correct method' that Marx
provides in the third section of that 1857 General Introduction of which Althusser makes so much (pp. 100–108).[8]
Here, briefly, Marx distinguishes, with reference to the
history of political economy, two moments of analysis. In the
first 'a small number of determinant, abstract, general
relations' are laboriously abstracted from 'the real and the
concrete'; in the second these relations (concepts) serve as the
basis for 'a reproduction of the concrete by way of thought'
(*ibid*, pp. 100–101). It is this second procedure which Marx
qualifies as 'scientifically correct'. And it is this qualification
which provides textual sanction for the Althusserian *aprio-
rism* expressed, at its extreme, in Balibar's attempt to generate the concepts of all possible modes of production by
permutating five 'formal invariants' (*Reading Capital*, pt. 3).[9]

I do not wish to engage in lengthy discussion of Marx's
1857 text here, having done so elsewhere (1979). On the other
hand, what many have taken to be Marx's most fundamental

discussion of method cannot simply be ignored. So first, let us be absolutely clear that *contra* Althusser, Marx nowhere in the Introduction denies the real ground of his 'simple abstractions'. On the contrary, he stresses it, with some force, against Hegel:

> The concrete . . . is the point of departure in reality and hence also the point of departure for observation and conception . . . [The] concrete in thought . . . [is] a product of the working up of observation and conception into concepts . . . Hence, in the theoretical method, too, the subject, society, must always be kept in mind as the presupposition (General Introduction, pp. 101–102).

The consistency of this with those 'empiricist' passages that I have quoted already, both pre- and post-1857, is manifest, and must raise grave doubts over the propriety of Althusser's attempt to legitimise his own view of concept formation by reference to Marx's observations in the Introduction. The 'simple abstractions' Marx speaks of as a starting point for reconstituting the concrete in thought are already products of a labour which is unmistakably *a posteriori*. I believe Althusser is a victim of a simple confusion here, and one Marx warned against in respect of *Capital*;

> Of course the method of presentation must differ in form from that of enquiry. The latter has to appropriate the material in detail, to analyze its different forms of development, to trace out their inner connection. Only after this work is done, can the actual movement be adequately described. If this is done successfully, if the life of the subject-matter is ideally reflected as in a mirror, then it may appear as if we had before us a mere *a priori* construction. (Afterword to second German edition of *Capital*, I, p. 19).[10]

Marx's admission of the empirical basis of the most 'abstract' of his categories and the text's overt preoccupation with their proper order of exposition both suggest that what Marx describes as scientifically correct is in fact a method of presentation rather than analysis.

Importantly, however, Marx in any case abandoned the categorial sequence mooted in September 1857 (see Nicolaus, Foreword to Marx's *Grundrisse*, pp. 36f). Both the 1859 *Critique* and *Capital* begin not with 'general, abstract deter-

minants which obtain in more or less all forms of society'
(*Grundrisse*, p. 108) as proposed in the plan with which Marx
concludes his 1857 disquisition, but with the '*concrete entity
the commodity*' (*Notes on Adolf Wagner*, p. 45). The probable
reasons for this change of strategy[11] make the hypothesis that
Marx's 1857 remarks accurately describe *Capital*'s method of
analysis (and in particular of concept formation) still less
tenable.

Here I must digress into an issue which will prove crucial
later in this paper. Between the drafting of the General
Introduction in 1857, and the publication of the first volume
of *Capital* a decade later, lie several important developments
in Marx's thought. For a start, it was only in the *Grundrisse*
that Marx for the first time formulated a non-Ricardian
theory of surplus value (see Mandel, *The Formation of the
Economic Thought of Karl Marx*). One such development
which has received less attention is of a methodological
order. In his 1857 text Marx noted, and worried around, an
ambiguity of reference in 'the simple abstractions' of political
economy. He exemplifies: 'This example of labour shows
strikingly how even the most abstract categories, despite
their validity – precisely because of their abstractness – for
all epochs, are nevertheless, in the specific character of this
abstraction, themselves likewise a product of historic relations, and possess their full validity only for and within these
relations (*Grundrisse*, p. 105)'. By 1867 Marx's hesitations had
disappeared. But so crucially had such ambiguous categories.
' "Labour as such", labour pure and simple' does not figure in
Capital's lexicon, and its occurrence in that of Ricardo occa-
sions Marx's censure (*Theories of Surplus Value*, pt. 2, p. 164).
Labour in *Capital*, is always qualified. The referents conflated
in the classical category now devolve on different concepts.
Those attributes which all human labour shares are subsumed
under the concept of useful labour; those qualities which
stamp it in any given case as being a particular social form of
labour (private, wage, slave, etc.) are apprehended through
equally particular categories (in the case of the labour discussed in the General Introduction, the category of abstract
labour). Marx insists, moreover, that the distinction between
useful and abstract labour is, in his own words, 'the pivot on

which a clear comprehension of Political Economy turns' (*Capital*, I, p. 41; see Letters to Engels, 24 August 1867 and 8 January 1868, *Selected Correspondence*). He is not splitting hairs.

The useful/abstract labour distinction is one instance of a general and systematic strategy in *Capital*, which is equally evident in Marx's distinctions of use-value and exchange-value, or technical composition and value composition of capital, and his criticisms of Smith on productive labour or Ricardo on fixed and circulating capital.[12] The Marx of 1867 scrupulously distinguishes what I shall refer to as historical and transhistorical categories.[13] Transhistorical categories are concepts which grasp features common to production in general, and hence may validly be applied across its various modes. Otherwise put, they are concepts for the classes of phenomena whose members are present in any production whatsoever. But as Marx knew in 1857,[14] '*production in general* is an abstraction' (*Grundrisse*, p. 85); the class does not exist independently of its members. Historical categories grasp those attributes of economic phenomena which distinguish them as belonging precisely to specific modes of production, or are in other words concepts of individual members of these classes. In Marx's terms, they are categories for the particular social forms in which the elements of production in general exist empirically.

This distinction renders the model of analysis Althusser and others derive from the General Introduction extremely problematic. Briefly, the 'simple abstractions' from which *Capital* allegedly departs must be unambiguously either transhistorical or historical categories. If taken to be the former will lead to the absurd position of trying to deduce a particular from a universal, the concept of a member of a class from the concept of the class. This procedure was one Marx roundly denounced in Hegel as far back as 1843.[15] On the other hand if the abstractions are regarded as historical there is no lesser problem. In this case there is the presupposition of the possession of precisely the adequate, non-ideological concepts whose formation are supposed to be explained; for manifestly, those categories in which phenomenal forms are spontaneously grasped, being subject to the opacity of those forms, cannot officiate as means for a scientifically adequate 'reproduction of the concrete by way of thought'. Unless the initial abstractions are regarded as purely arbitrary constructs, one is forced inexorably back to Marx's first moment of analysis, wherein categories are abstracted from the concrete, as the critical locus of his concept formation.

IV

I have sought to suggest that contrary to the Althusserian account, Marx does conceive his science in terms of unearthing the 'essence' of the real from the forms in which one experiences it, the corollary being that scientific concepts[16] are constructed *a posteriori* by abstraction from these forms. But clearly there must be more to this abstraction than the simple 'extraction' of the essential from the inessential among empirically given elements which Althusser satirizes. For Marx, as already observed, phenomenal forms may disguise the relations they express; in consequence constructs built upon phenomenal categories (like, say, the Weberian ideal-type) cannot be regarded as scientifically adequate concepts of these underlying relations.

Marx's abstraction therefore takes the form not of 'extraction', as Althusser conceives it, but of what I shall term a critique. From the *Kritik des hegelschen Staatsrecht* of 1843 to the *Kritik der Politischen Oekonomie* which dominated his mature years[17] Marx persistently described his work thus. Colletti (Introduction to *Karl Marx: Early Writings*) has drawn interesting methodological parallels between these 'early' and 'late' writings which merit further investigation. He is also one of the few to have remarked on the specificially Kantian ancestry of the concept within the classical German philosophical tradition in which Marx was reared (*Marxism and Hegel*, ch. 8, 'Marxism and the Dialectic').[18] Clearly Marx was no Kantian; his typical assertion that 'the logical categories are coming damn well out of "our intercourse"' after all' (Letter to Engels, 25 March 1868, *Selected Correspondence*) represents a denial of all Kant held central to his Copernican Revolution. There is nonetheless, I shall argue, a striking analogy between their critical methods.

For Kant, a critique was more than a mere 'criticism of books and systems'. It was a definite form of analysis: one which located the conditions of 'possibility or impossibility', and thereby the 'origin . . . extent and limits' of its object (Preface to *Critique of Pure Reason*, p. 3), in Kant's case, a scientific metaphysics. Kant referred to his analysis of conditions as a transcendental analytic and his ensuing determination of limits as a transcendental dialectic. Both, in my view, have their strict counterparts in Marx. Briefly, Marx's object is the social forms assumed by economic phenomena (or, *mutatis mutandis*, stateforms). His 'analytic' consists in an excavation of the conditions that must be supposed for the phenomena to assume such forms, that is, of the essential relations that must exist if the world as experienced is to be possible. Marx's reasoning is thus eminently transcendental, though *pace* Kant his is a transcendental realism. His 'dialectic', finally (and arguably this is the only sense in which this slippery term can usefully be applied to his work), involves defining the limits within which the categories which grasp these forms can validly be applied, and thence evaluating theories and explanations, like those of bourgeois political economy, which rest upon such categories. With this overview in mind, let me now elaborate in procedural terms.[19]

V

I spoke above of changes in Marx's starting-point after September 1857. What was to become the opening of both the 1859 *Critique* and *Capital* is definitively announced at the very end of the *Grundrisse*: 'the first category in which bourgeois wealth presents itself is that of the *commodity*' (*Grundrisse*, p. 881). Marx goes on, as he later does in *Capital*, to distinguish two aspects of the commodity, use-value and exchange-value. The terms in which he draws this distinction leave no doubts as to his object of enquiry. Of use-value he comments,

> This is its [the commodity's] material side, which the most disparate epochs of production may have in common, and whose examination

therefore lies beyond political economy. [. . .] What it is customary
to say about it in general terms, for the sake of good form, is confined
to commonplaces which had a historic value in the first beginnings of
the science, when the social forms of bourgeois production had still
laboriously to be peeled out of the material, and, at great effort, to be
established as independent objects of study. *(ibid)*.

The point is reiterated at the start of the 1859 *Critique*. Here,
Marx further emphasizes that 'use-values . . . do not express
the social relations of production' (Preface to *Critique*, p. 28).
Exchange-value is, by contrast, 'a determinate economic
form' *(ibid)*, that is precisely an expression of the 'specific
economic relation . . . which stamps the use-value as a
commodity' (*Grundrisse*, p. 881). It is 'not only the most
abstract, but is also the most universal form, taken by the
product in bourgeois production, and stamps that production
as a particular species of social production, and thereby
gives it its special historical character' (*Capital*, I, p. 80).

It is this universality of the commodity-form (within the
relations of bourgeois production) which renders the commodity rather than, say, money or capital, Marx's particular
starting-point; the latter are developments of the commodity-
form itself that suppose its conditions to obtain.[20] This is,
perhaps, a presentational refinement, a beginning finally
settled only after extensive analysis had already been undertaken; the *Grundrisse* actually begins with money and works
back to the commodity. But what is significant in the fore-
going passages, for my purposes, is the analytic strategy they
display irrespective of the particular social form at issue.
This is clear and unambiguous.

The first act of Marx's critique is rigorously to disentangle
those attributes which the phenomena under investigation
have in common with their counterparts in other modes of
production from those attributes which define these phenomena as specific social forms. To employ the terms I introduced above, Marx distinguishes qualities which phenomena
exhibit as elements of production in general, class attributes
grasped by transhistorical categories, from qualities which
differentiate such phenomena as individual members of
classes, capable of being apprehended only via historical
categories. The former are put on one side; but the latter form

the object of further analysis.[21] Marx exemplifies in respect of the commodity:

> I analyze this, and, indeed, first in *the form in which it appears*. Here I find that on the one hand it is in its natural form . . . a *use-value*, on the other hand . . . 'exchange-value'. Further analysis of the latter shows me that exchange-value is a 'phenomenal *form*', an independent mode of representation of the *value* contained in the commodity, and then I proceed to analyze the latter. (Notes on Adolf Wagner, p. 50).

There is, one should note, an important sense in which 'general, abstract determinants' (though in this case properly transhistorical categories rather than the ambiguous 'simple abstractions' of classical economy[22]) do serve Marx as a kind of 'starting-point'. But it is not the Althusserian sense; Marx repeatedly makes clear that such concepts are 'abstract moments with which no real historical stage of production can be grasped' (*Grundrisse*, p. 88). As argued above, their nature as class concepts precludes their playing the role that, say, Balibar envisages. However, formally speaking, Marx needs already to have identified the constituents of production in general in order first, to isolate a set of phenomena as pertaining to production in any given empirical case, and second, to distinguish, within these phenomena, such attributes as are not predicates of the classes to which they belong. The analysis of production in general is therefore logically prior[23] to that of its particular modes. It must be clear, however, that its role here[24] is simply one of furnishing Marx with his empirical *explananda*. Possession of transhistorical categories enables Marx only to identify phenomena as productive and to isolate those attributes which are not explicable by the requisites of production in general. The most significant theoretical labour is yet to come.

The next step in Marx's critique is to explain why the phenomena he has thus identified should take such forms. Since the latter are defined precisely by attributes not common to production in general, they are not explicable by its exigencies. They are on the contrary 'phenomenal forms of essential relations' specific to the modes of production in which they occur, or in other words suppose a 'material groundwork or set of conditions of existence' (*Capital*, I, pp. 537, 80) which is historical. It is this Marx now sets out to unearth, and 'unearthing' is the appropriate metaphor. For, as already observed, in Marx's view phenomenal forms are apt to mislead. Forms and relations need no visible connection while manifest correlations may be spurious. Thus, for instance, the exploitation which links profit to the separation of labour from the means of production which is its *sine qua non* is not a manifest feature of capitalist production; the correlation of wages to work done, on the other hand, is massively apparent (in all senses).[25] Marx cannot therefore proceed by induction.

What he in effect does is to postulate mechanisms which should they exist would explain how the phenomena under investigation come to assume the forms in which they are experienced. He then treats the conditions necessary for the functioning of these mechanisms as the material groundwork of the forms themselves. To elaborate on this I shall draw on Hanson's work on what he calls the logic of scientific discovery.[26] Hanson argues, against the hypothetico-deductive school, that there is such a logic and that it takes what he terms a retroductive form. He schematizes the retroductive inference an follows:

(1) Some surprising phenomenon P is observed.
(2) P would be explicable as a matter of course if H were true.
(3) Hence there is reason to think H is true.
   (*Patterns of Discovery*, p. 86).[27]

Obviously retroduction cannot establish certainty, for some hypothesis other than H might be equally capable of explaining P. Hanson's point, however, is not that explanatory hypotheses do not require independent testing, but that, *pace* hypothetico-deductive theorists, their initial proposal is capable of rational description. First, the scientist does not reason blindly but always from a given set of phenomena;[28] 'The critical moment comes when the physicist perceives that ... one might explain this welter of phenomena P, throw it all into an intelligible pattern, by supposing H to obtain. *But P controls H, not vice versa.* The reasoning is from data to hypotheses and theories, not the reverse' (*ibid*, p. 88).

I should add here that this does not amount to a simple empiricism. Hanson makes clear that 'the astonishment may consist in the fact the p is at variance with existing *theories*' (*ibid*, p. 81n). This is clearly how Marx sees the issue, as will be apparent from my discussion of his criticisms of Ricardo below. Second, despite its non-apodictic character, retroductive reasoning has what Hanson considers a definite logical form. A putative H must satisfy strict criteria of adequacy; principally,[29] a requirement of consistency among its component propositions, and a requirement of what I shall term exhaustiveness; 'the hypothesis cannot be admitted, even as a tentative conjecture, unless it would account for the phenomena posing the difficulty . . . ' (*ibid*, p. 86).

Now, whatever its merits as an account of the logic of scientific discovery *per se*, I believe that Hanson's description more than adequately fits the inferential procedures of Marx's 'analytic'. I have already argued both that Marx must reason *a posteriori* from phenomenal forms to essential relations, and that this reasoning, is not inductive but (to quote Peirce's words on retroduction) 'amounts to . . . observing a fact and then professing to say what . . . it was that gave rise to that fact' (Hanson, *Patterns of Discovery*, p. 89). It remains to show that Marx's inferences conform to Hanson's criteria of adequacy.

No special demonstration of Marx's concern with consistency need be provided here; it is manifestly central to his entire critique of classical economy and in particular of classical theories of surplus-value.[30] His simultaneous commitment to the requirement of exhaustiveness, on the other hand, has seldom been remarked, though it is no less fundamental to that same critique.[31] This may briefly be illustrated by various of his comments on Ricardo.

A famous passage in *Theories of Surplus Value* praises classical political economy for its attempt to,

> reduce the various . . . forms of wealth to their inner unity by means of analysis and to strip away the form in which they exist independently alongside one another. It seeks to grasp the inner connection in contrast to the multiplicity of outward forms.

But, Marx continues,

It often attempts directly, leaving out the intermediate links, to carry through the reduction and to prove that the various forms are derived from one and the same source. (*Theories of Surplus Value*, pt. 3, p. 500).

Ricardo, for instance, directly (and illegitimately[32]) identifies natural price with value, and profit with surplus-value. Marx focuses his objections in the following, rather dense, observation:

Ricardo ... consciously *abstracts* from the form of competition, from the appearance of competition, in order to comprehend the *laws as such*. On the one hand he must be reproached for not going far enough, for not carrying his abstraction to completion ... On the other hand one must reproach him for regarding the phenomenal form as *immediate and direct* proof or exposition of the general laws ... In regard to the first, his abstraction is too incomplete; in regard to the second, it is formal abstraction which in itself is wrong. (*Theories of Surplus Value*, pt. 2, p. 106).

This double error of on the one hand 'incomplete', and on the other hand 'formal', or as Marx describes it elsewhere (*Capital*, I, p. 307), 'violent abstraction', is a recurrent motif of Marx's Ricardian criticism.[33]

What these charges amount to is this. To abstract violently involves immediately identifying phenomena with their alleged essences without an adequate specification of the mechanisms through which the latter manifest themselves in the former, or, to use a different terminology, treating the phenomena as direct instantiations of laws which in fact operate only in mediate fashion. The consequence is that there remains an empirical residuum which resists consistent explanation, and has to be either dismissed as 'inessential' or subsumed under further more or less *ad hoc* hypotheses. In Ricardo's case, for instance, the mechanisms which explain why, under capitalist conditions, natural price should deviate from value and profit from surplus-value remain unexplicated, and Ricardo is ultimately driven to posit alternative determinants of value in order to handle the resulting empirical difficulties.[34] Marx comments: 'The vulgar mob has therefore concluded that theoretical truths are abstractions which are at variance with reality, instead of seeing, on the contrary, that Ricardo does not carry true abstract thinking far enough ... ' (*Theories of Surplus Value*, pt. 2, p. 437). This is a direct appeal to the criterion of exhaustiveness; 'true abstract thinking', we must infer, consists in developing the *explanans* up to the point where the refractory empirical residuum disappears. Here, for instance,

> Instead of *postulating* this *general rate of profit*, Ricardo should rather have examined in how far its *existence* is in fact consistent with the determination of value by labour-time, and he would have found that instead of being consistent with it, *prima facie* it *contradicts* it, and that its existence would have to be explained through a number of intermediary stages, a procedure which is very different from merely including it under the law of value. He would then have gained an altogether different insight into the nature of profit and would not have identified it directly with surplus-value. (*ibid*, p. 174).

Satisfaction of retroductive criteria, as I have indicated above, cannot of course guarantee certainty; though it must be conceded, I think, that to produce a consistent explanation of the range of phenomena Marx deals with in *Capital* is no mean achievement. Elsewhere, I have endeavoured to show that Marx's *explanans* is open in principle to independent empirical testing.[35] Here, however, I wish only to emphasize, against the Althusserians, the centrality of the empirical to its formulation. For Marx, as for Hanson, 'P controls H, not vice versa'.

Having thus retroduced mechanisms capable of explaining how the phenomena under analysis can assume the forms in which we observe them, Marx takes the conditions which themselves explain why such mechanisms should exist as the essential relations behind the forms in question. The possibility of products assuming the value-form, for instance, is explained by their commensurability as repositories of abstract labour (*Capital*, I, pp. 40–70; Appendix to 1st edition of *Capital*, I), while 'why labour is represented by the value of its product and labour-time by the magnitude of that value' (*Capital*, I, p. 80) is explained in turn by the relations peculiar to commodity production (*ibid*, pp. 71–83).[36] In the same way, the possibility of the profit which phenomenally defines the capital-form is explained by the exchange of labour-power against variable capital and the production of surplus-value in its consumption, and the existence of such mechanisms by the 'double freedom' of the labourer.

This finally enables Marx to construct adequate historical categories. Phenomenal forms (of which it was only known *that* they were historical at the outset of the critique) can now be reconceptualized in terms of their precise historical conditions of existence, as forms of manifestation of historically specific essential relations. Thus Marx writes for instance that the 'severance of the conditions of production on the one hand, from the producers, on the other . . . forms the *conception* of capital' (*Capital*, III, p. 246, my emphasis). Otherwise put, capital is revealed, and thereafter conceptually apprehended not as the thing it initially appeared to be but as 'a definite social production relation, belonging to a definite historical formation of society, which is manifested in a thing and lends this thing a specific social character' (*ibid*, p. 814).

VI

What I have termed Marx's 'dialectic' flows directly from here. As we have seen Marx posits a relation of correspondence between forms of experience and categories of thought. The categories of bourgeois economy, for example, are for him 'forms of thought expressing with social validity the conditions and relations of a definite, historically determined mode of production' (even though *that* they are such need by no means be immediately apparent[37]) (*Capital*, I, p. 76). Hence, to have determined the conditions of existence of a given set of phenomenal forms is *a fortiori* to delimit the boundaries within which the categories through which these forms are spontaneously apprehended can properly be applied. Marx's dialectic, briefly, consists in reassessing the validity or otherwise of existing explanations of the same phenomena in the light of this criterion. Its force will best be appreciated if I say something about its targets.

A central feature of specifically bourgeois ideology, in Marx's view, is what he calls its fetishism. *Capital* introduces this latter notion via a well-known analogy with 'the mist-enveloped regions of the religious world', in which 'the productions of the human brain appear as independent beings endowed with life, and entering into relation both with one another and the human race. So it is in the world of commodities with the products of men's hands' (*ibid*, p. 72). Elsewhere Marx is more specific. 'The fetishism peculiar to the capitalist mode of production from which it arises', he writes, 'consists in regarding *economic* categories, such as being a *commodity* or *productive* labour, as qualities inherent in the material incarnations of these formal determinations or categories' (*Capital*, I, p. 1046). '[It] metamorphoses the social, economic character impressed on things in the process of social production into a natural character stemming from the material nature of those things' (*Capital*, II, p. 229). Let me elaborate.[38]

We have previously seen that Marx distinguishes the 'material side' of economic phenomena, that is attributes they share with their counterparts in all modes of production, from qualities which define them as determinate economic or social forms. Only the former can be explained by the exigencies of production in general; the latter derive from, and must be explained by, essential relations specific to the modes of production in which they occur. But a fetishized discourse systematically confuses these attributes in what amounts to a double inversion. First, properties which phenomena exhibit solely as a result of their standing in some definite set of social relations are wrongly regarded an emanations of their 'material side'. Price, for instance, is fetishistically explained by use-value, or profit by the role of the means of production in the labour-process. Second, thus to explain the social by the natural is *ipso facto* to universalize the historical. Here as elsewhere Marx insists that there is more involved than 'pure subjective illusion which conceals the deceit and the interests of the exploiting classes'. As *Capital* abundantly exemplifies,[39] 'the way of looking at things arises out of the relationship itself; the latter is an expression of the former, not vice versa' (*Theories of Surplus Value*, pt. 3, p. 296). Fetishistic illusions concerning value, for instance, are readily sustained by the fact that the value of any one commodity is phenomenally evident only in the shape of some definite physical quantity of another (*Capital*, I, p. 47f; Appendix to 1st edition of *Capital*, I). Nevertheless fetishism is eminently convenient for the ruling classes. For its net effect is to translate the complex facts of capitalism into the simple facts of life. The world men and women have constructed confronts its creators as an independent and immutable *datum* before whose brute facticity they can but acquiesce.

Otherwise put, fetishism involves a two-fold transgression of proper categorial boundaries. On the one hand, properties which distinguish phenomena as individual members of classes and hence ought properly to be the object of historical categories are subsumed under transhistorical categories and explained by theses logically capable of accounting only for characteristics of the classes to which they belong. The trinity formula of vulgar economics, for example, links three elements of production in general (land, labour, and means of production) with three determinate economic forms (rent, wages, and interest[40]) in just such a spurious causal correlation. Marx refers to these as 'incommensurable magnitudes' (*Capital*, III, p. 823). And on the other hand, the historical attributes of the phenomena are thereby falsely universalized. In the trinity formula, for instance, the capacity of bourgeois property to command ground-rent is transmuted into an attribute of land *per se*. Clearly, having established the historicity of social forms through his analytic, Marx can readily detect both such errors.

I will end this discussion by emphasizing the subversiveness of this dialectic. This is also the appropriate place to return to the Althusserians. In 1966 *Reading Capital* argued, correctly, that Marxism is no historicism.[41] A decade later Hindess and Hirst, in characteristically provocative fashion, went further and asserted the study of history to be 'not only scientifically but also politically valueless' and denied any necessary or worthwhile connection between Marxism and the historian's craft (*Pre-Capitalist Modes of Production*, pp. 312, 308). Marx, I think, would have dissented. Certainly his critique as I have outlined it here is not of itself an historical analysis. But in Marx's own words,

our method indicates the points where historical investigation must enter in ... In order to develop the laws of bourgeois economy ... it is not necessary to write the *real history of the relations of production*. But the correct observation and deduction of these laws ... always leads to primary equations ... which point towards a past lying behind this system. These indications ... then also offer the key to the understanding of the past ... (*Grundrisse*, pp. 460–1).

Marx's critique, by exposing the historicity of the phenomena which it treats and the bankruptcy of accounts which violate this historicity, accomplishes, to use a favourite Althusserian metaphor, a radical shift of terrain. Fetishism, as already seen, presents a dehistoricized, desocialized world whose makers are reduced to passive spectators in a mystery not of their making. Marx's critique points behind this, *to* a history. Once capital, for instance, has been revealed as supposing a relation of exploitation via the wage contract, then it is known where its origins must be sought, not in the abstemious habits of early Puritans but in the class struggles which secured 'a Decomposition of the Original Union existing between the Labouring Man and his Instruments of Labour' (*Wages, Price and Profit*, p. 45). It is here that the shift of terrain lies; precisely in unmasking the apparently authorless theatre of fetishism as an intensely *human* drama. And it is here too that we touch on another theme dear to Marx and reviled by the Althusserians; that of human self-alienation and its overcoming.[42]

This real history can only be recovered using all the tools of the historian's craft, and therein lies their scientific value. Part 8 of *Capital* represents an incisive, if sketchy, essay and at the least should serve to indicate the intimacy with which Marx linked the analytic and the historical sides of his investigations. As regards the political value of the history whose possibility Marx's critique heralds, I will let Marx speak for himself:

from the moment that the bourgeois mode of production and the conditions of production and distribution which correspond to it are recognized as *historical*, the delusion of regarding them as natural laws of production vanishes and the prospect opens up of a new society, [a new] economic social formation, to which capitalism is only the transition. (*Theories of Surplus Value*, p. 429).

VII

Althusserianism (of which, for these purposes, Hindess and Hirst may be taken as providing the most consistent elaboration) links, in a more or less systematic fashion, a conventionalist epistemology, an *aprioristic* methodology, and a repudiation of history. This *mélange* is well-known and regrettably influential. In this paper I have sought to reveal a radically different set of connections: between a materialist epistemology, a methodology governed by strict criteria of empirical adequacy, and a recognition of the centrality of history to social theory and socialist practice. Ill as they may accord with fashionable philosophies of science, it was the latter which gave us *Capital*.

Notes

1. Althusser's retreats began with his *Lenin and Philosophy*; see Balibar, 'Self-Criticism', Rancière, 'On the theory of ideology: the politics of Althusser'. The British disciples I refer to are those of the former *Theoretical Practice* group, above all Hindess and Hirst. The latter, of course, have broken with *Reading Capital*'s positions on a number of issues – see especially their *Pre-Capitalist Modes* and *Mode of Production and Social Formation* – but not, in general, those discussed in this paper.

2. Althusser is somewhat vague in his original specification of G2. His qualification in his *For Marx*, p. 184 n2 includes 'technique' as well as concepts under the rubric of 'theory'. But the 'much more serious examination' he promises there never materializes.

3. In their *Mode of Production*, pp. 46f Hindess and Hirst go beyond even this position to expunge the category of 'the concrete' entirely: 'Social formation . . . is a *concept* . . . The concept of a determinate social formation is not the appropriation in thought of an independently existing "concrete" social formation' (ibid, p. 48). Althusser himself does not tell us where G2 concepts come from, only that they are not abstractions from the real object; the programme developed by Balibar in *Reading Capital*, however, has an emphatically *a priori* character. This latter is discussed briefly below.

4. Althusserians would not accept this characterization. Hindess' *Mode of Production* commences with a repudiation of epistemological discourse as such. To my mind problems do not disappear simply because one chooses to ignore them. Ironically, Hirst was one of the first to point to the inconsistency entailed in Althusser's attempt to provide himself with transcendent guarantees of truth via the concept of 'theory' – see his 'Althusser and Philosophy'. Hirst however failed to draw out the obvious implications for the science/ideology distinction, holding at that time that Althusser had remedied the lacuna in his *Lenin and Philosophy*, and that it had no repercussions for the rest of his system. Subsequently Hindess and Hirst have rejected the possibility of any universal science/ideology distinction; *Mode of Production*, pp. 30–3.

5. Marx, *Grundrisse*, pp. 100–2; see his Afterword to second German edition of *Capital*, I, pp. 19–20, where the charge is repeated.

6. This again is ironic, in so far as this text not only makes Marx's materialism with regard to concepts very clear, but also, as I argue below, characterizes *Capital*'s process of concept formation as emphatically *a posteriori*. As the accompanying note made clear, the main interest of these Notes for the Althusserians lay in their alleged 'anti-humanism'.

49

7 I refer to Godelier in *Ideology in Social Science*, Geras, *ibid*, Cohen, 'Karl Marx and the withering away of Social Science' and Mepham, 'The theory of ideology in *Capital*'. My *Marx's Method* ch. 1 rehearses these arguments; chs. 2 and 3 illustrate them at length with reference to Marx's analyses of value and the trinity formula.

8 After *Capital*, this text has the single largest number of entries in the index to *Reading Capital* for any work by Marx. It is fundamental to Althusser's epistemological position; see *Reading Capital*, pp. 40–1, 46–8, and pt. 1 *passim*.

9 Balibar claims that 'the distinction between different modes is necessarily and *sufficiently* based' on these invariants (Althusser, *Reading Capital*, p. 225). On the next page he qualifies this (somewhat obscurely) and tells us that he is speaking only of the 'pertinences' of historical analysis: 'an essential intermediate step in the determination of the historical forms taken by labour-power, property, "real appropriation", etc'. *How* these 'pertinences' aid the construction of such historical concepts is *not* specified; the obvious risk, in an Althusserian perspective, is one of 'empiricism' entering here by the back door. Hindess and Hirst, in *Pre-Capitalist Modes of Production*, are less sanguine; for them, the concepts of modes of production are *a priori* constructs whose validity is completely independent of any empirical or historical reference (pp. 1–5, 320–3).

10 Althusser in fact discusses this distinction of Marx's in *Reading Capital*, pp. 49–50, assimilating the method of presentation here to the method of analysis Marx speaks of in his Preface to first German edition of *Capital*, I. As regards Marx's method of enquiry, Althusser merely notes that its 'protocols . . . are contained in part in his notebooks', *without* elaborating. If I am correct in contending that Marx's critical concepts are constructed *a posteriori* in the course of the latter, Althusser's silence here must be judged a serious lacuna in a text purporting to offer a methodological commentary.

11 Marx's comments on the intimacy of the connection between what he terms the 'faulty architectonics' of Ricardo's presentation and errors in his 'method of investigation' are pertinent here: *Theories of Surplus Value*, pt. 2, pp. 164–7.

12 On Smith, see Marx, *Theories of Surplus Value*, pt. 1, ch. 4, secs 3 and 4; on Ricardo, *Capital*, II, ch. 11.

13 I should stress here that the distinction pertains to the *reference* of the categories. For Marx all categories are historical inasmuch as definite historical conditions are required for their *production*. See his *Grundrisse*, pp. 100–8, and his remarks on Aristotle in his *Capital*, I, pp. 59–60.

14 Unfortunately *this* section of the 1857 Introduction, which argues *inter alia* that 'the so-called *general preconditions* of all production are nothing more than . . . abstract moments with which no real historical stage of production can be grasped' (*Grundrisse*, p. 88) has largely been ignored by the Althusserians. The reasons why Marx did

not use the 1857 Introduction are relevant to the case I argue here: see his Preface to the *Critique*, p. 19.

15 See his *Contribution to the Critique of Hegel's Philosophy of Law*, pp. 12–14.

16 Subject to the qualification expressed in note 22 below.

17 Marx described the *Grundrisse* as a 'critique of the economic categories' (Letter to Lassalle, 1858, *Selected Correspondence*). Its twice-revised first chapter was published in 1859 under the title *Zur Kritik der Politischen Oekonomie* (*A Contribution to the Critique of Political Economy*). This was also the title he gave his vast Ms of 1861–3, which contained a full first draft of vol. I of *Capital*, preliminary discussions of topics later to be considered in vols II and III, and the whole of *Theories of Surplus Value*. When published, *Capital* bore the same sub-title.

18 I expand on this in my 'Some issues in historical materialism' pp. 141–3.

19 I do not mean to imply by this that I am setting up a methodological 'recipe' or prescription. Rather, I aim to provide a retrospective formal account of what Althusser would call the 'protocols' of Marx's analysis.

20 It is this that allows Marx to present the development of money and capital from the commodity in vol. I in quasi-Hegelian fashion. See Nicolaus, Foreword to Marx's *Grundrisse*, sec. 3. See Marx, Afterword to second German edition of *Capital*, I.

21 Transhistorical attributes enter into the sphere of political economy, Marx qualifies, if and insofar as they themselves become 'determinate form(s)' (Preface to *Critique*, p. 28). An example might be the use-value of labour-power in the theory of surplus-value.

22 The 'simple abstractions' Marx speaks of in his 1857 Introduction include value, money, and exchange-value, that is eminently historical categories.

23 As mentioned in note 12 above, and argued in sec. 2 of this paper, there is a sense in which for Marx *all* categories are historical. In practice, one would expect the distinction between what pertains to production in general and what pertains to the mode under analysis to emerge only in the course of enquiry.

24 Elsewhere it plays a larger role, furnishing lawlike propositions which officiate as premises in explanation. See, for example, the justification of his theory of value Marx offers in his Letter to Kugelmann.

25 See Marx, *Capital*, I, pt. 6 *passim*; Geras in *Ideology in Social Science*; Sayer, 'Some issues in historical materialism': pp. 86–8; *Marx's method*, ch. 3, sec. 2(c).

26 For elaboration see Hanson, *Patterns of Discovery*, 'The logic of discovery', 'More on the logic of discovery', 'Retroduction and the logic of scientific discovery'.

27 Hanson gives a more guarded variant in his 'Retroduction and the logic of scientific discovery': pp. 81–2.

28 I am not supposing a neutral observation language here; phenomena, as I use the term, means things-as-experienced. Marx simply *assumes* a correspondence of language to phenomenal forms, as explained above. I believe Althusser is right here to see Marx's starting-point as extant descriptions (G1), though given the assumption of correspondence it can make no difference whether we take the object as the descriptions themselves or their purported referents.

29 Hanson lists a third criterion, which I argue ('Some issues in historical materialism', pp. 164–70; *Marx's Method*, ch. 5, sec. 2(b)) Marx also adheres to: 'If H is meant to explain P, then H cannot itself rest on the features in P which required explanation' (*Grundrisse*, p. 88).

30 For a summary, see Engels, Introduction to *Marx's Wage-Labour and Capital*.

31 I exemplify this in detail in my 'Some issues in historical materialism', pp. 150–64; *Marx's Method*, ch. 5, sec. 2(b).

32 For Marx, in a capitalist economy (as opposed to simple commodity production) if one assumes a uniform rate of surplus value (s/v) rates of profit $(s/(v + c))$ on different capitals will vary with their organic compositions (c/v). Capital will ordinarily migrate in search of highest rates of profit, that is to sectors with below-average organic composition, and this will result in imbalances of supply and demand and ensuing deviations of prices from values. The net effect, according to Marx, will be the establishment of an average rate of profit, equivalent to that on a capital of average social composition. In consequence, the normal or 'natural' selling price of products of capitals with above-average or below-average compositions will deviate from their values, and the profit they realize will differ accordingly from the surplus-value they actually embody. See *Capital*, III, pts 1 and 2.

33 It is particularly worth remarking this in view of Althusser's implied contention, in his *Reading Capital*, pt. 1, that the use of appearance/essence distinctions *per se* involves recourse to an implicit category of the 'inessential real'.

34 See Ricardo, *Principles of Political Economy and Taxation*, ch. 1, secs. 4 and 5; for Marx's comment, see his *Theories of Surplus Value*, pt. 2, p. 191, and more generally his criticisms of the 'scholasticism' of Mill *et al.* in his *Theories of Surplus Value*, pt. 3, ch. 20.

35 By both comparison and prediction. See my 'Some issues in historical materialism', pp. 170–83; *Marx's Method*, ch. 5, sec. 3.

36 Marx, *Selected Correspondence*, ought also to be referred to here, together with Marx's critique of Samuel Bailey in his *Theories of Surplus Value*, pt. 3, pp. 133f.

37 See the famous paragraph beginning 'Man's reflections . . .', on the page before that from which this quotation is taken.

38 On fetishism, see, further, Colletti, 'Bernstein and the Marxism of the Second International', pp. 82–92, Rubin, *Essays on Marx's Theory of Value*, pt. 1.

39 See my 'Some issues in historical materialism', ch. 1, pts 2 and 3; *Marx's Method*, chs. 2 and 3.

40 Marx discusses the trinity formula in his *Theories of Surplus Value*, pt. 3, Addenda, and *Capital*, III, ch. 48. In the earlier text he first discusses profit as the apparent revenue of 'capital' (*qua* means of production) but soon concludes that 'it is interest, not profit, which appears to be the creation of value arising from capital as such' (*Theories of Surplus Value*, pt. 3, p. 462) and thereafter discusses the relevant relation as capital-interest. In the resulting trinity formula, profit (of enterprise) becomes subsumed under the relation labour-wages, as a 'wage' for the capitalist's 'labour'.

41 I also argue this, though on different grounds from Althusser, in my 'Method and dogma in historical materialism'.

42 This debate lies beyond the concerns of this paper; but Colletti makes out a cogent case, directed against both the Althusserians and their more 'humanist' opponents, for believing that the notion of human essence (and *a fortiori* the theory of alienation) in Marx's *early* writings do not suppose the 'philosophical anthropology' which both camps find there.

Bibliography

Althusser, L., 'On the materialist dialectic', in his *For Marx* (Harmondsworth 1969).

——, and E. Balibar, *Reading Capital* (London 1970).

——, *Lenin and Philosophy and other essays.* (London 1971).

Balibar, E., 'Self-criticism', *Theoretical Practice* 7/8, 1973.

Blackburn, R. (ed.), *Ideology in Social Science* (London 1972).

Cohen, G., 'Karl Marx and the withering away of social science', *Philosophy and Public Affairs*, I, 1972.

Colletti, L., 'Bernstein and the Marxism of the Second International', in his *From Rousseau to Lenin* (London 1972).

——, *Marxism and Hegel* (London 1973).

——, Introduction to *Karl Marx: Early Writings* (Harmondsworth 1975).

——, 'Marxism and the dialectic', *New Left Review*, 93, 1975.

Engels, F., Introduction to Marx's *Wage-Labour and Capital*.

Geras, N., 'Marx and the critique of political economy', in *Ideology in Social Science*, R. Blackburn (ed.) (1972).

Godelier, M., 'Structure and contradiction in *Capital*', *ibid.*

Hanson, N.R., *Patterns of Discovery* (Cambridge 1969).

——, 'The logic of discovery', *Journal of Philosophy*, LV, p. 25, 1958.

——, 'More on the logic of discovery', *Journal of Philosophy*, LVII, p. 6, 1960.

——, 'Retroduction and the logic of scientific discovery', in L. Krimerman (ed.), *The Nature and Scope of Social Science* (New York 1961).

Hindess, B. and P. Hirst, *Pre-Capitalist Modes of Production* (London 1975).

——, and P. Hirst, *Mode of Production and Social Formation* (London 1977).

Hirst, P., 'Althusser and Philosophy', *Theoretical Practice*, 2, 1971.

Kant, I., Preface to his *Critique of Pure Reason* (London 1969).

Mandel, E., *The Formation of the Economic Thought of Karl Marx* (London 1971).

Marx, K. and Engels, F., *Selected Correspondence* (Moscow 1956).

Marx, K., *Contribution to the Critique of Hegel's Philosophy of Law*, *Collected Works*, III.

——, and F. Engels, *The German Ideology* (Moscow 1965).

——, Letter to Annenkov with *The Poverty of Philosophy*.

——, *The Poverty of Philosophy* (New York 1973).

——, *Wage-Labour and Capital* (Moscow 1974).

——, General Introduction [to the *Grundrisse*], in his *Grundrisse*.

——, *Grundrisse* (Harmondsworth 1973).

——, Letter to Lassalle, Feb. 22, 1858, *Selected Correspondence*.

——, *A Contribution to the Critique of Political Economy* (London 1971).

——, *Theories of Surplus Value*, pts 1–3 (Moscow 1969–72).

——, *Capital*, III (Moscow 1971).

——, *Wages, Price and Profit* (Peking 1973).

——, 'Results of the immediate process of production', with *Capital*, I (Harmondsworth, 1976).

——, *Capital*, I (London 1970).

——, Letter to Engels, 27 June 1867, *Selected Correspondence*.

——, Letter to Engels, 27 August 1867. *Selected Correspondence*.

——, 'The form of value', Appendix to 1st edn. of *Capital*, I, in A. Dragstedt (ed.), *Value : Studies by Karl Marx* (New York 1976).

——, Letter to Engels, 8 January 1868, *Selected Correspondence*.

——, Letter to Engels, 25 March 1868, *Selected Correspondence*.

——, *Capital*, II (Moscow 1967).

——, Marginal Notes on Adolf Wagner's *Lehrbuch der Politischen Oekonomie*, *Theoretical Practice*, 5 (1972).

Mepham, J., 'The theory of ideology in *Capital*', *Radical Philosophy*, II, 1972, reprinted in this Volume.

Nicolaus, M., Foreword to Marx's *Grundrisse*.

Rancière, J., 'On the theory of Ideology: The politics of Althusser', *Radical Philosophy*, VII, 1974.

Ricardo, D., *Principles of Political Economy and Taxation* (London 1971).

Rubin, I., *Essays on Marx's Theory of Value* (Detroit 1972).

Sayer, D., 'Method and dogma in historical materialism', *Sociological Review*, XXIII, 1975. p. 4.

——, 'Some issues in historical materialism', PhD thesis, University of Durham, 1975.

——, *Marx's Method, Ideology, Science and Critique in 'Capital'* (Hassocks 1979).

In Defence of Epistemology
ANDREW COLLIER

MY aim in this paper is to criticize two post-Althusserian texts which urge us to ditch the whole project of epistemology; I shall also say something about the conditions for an epistemology which will not lay itself open to the objections raised against epistemology in these texts, in so far as those objections are valid. And I shall make some brief comments about some of the outstanding problems for an epistemology which is to cope with the human sciences – problems which are not made to disappear, but merely evaded, by the rejection of epistemology.

My task is therefore a polemical one – the defence of what I regard as already established positions of materialist epistemology, against new versions of idealism, albeit shame-faced (or as they say in the trade, 'de-negated') versions.[1]

The first book I shall consider is *Althusser's Marxism* by Alex Callinicos – an excellent book in many ways, written from the standpoint of a rigorously scientific and revolutionary Marxism, yet one which, on this crucial issue of epistemology, opens the floodgates of idealism. Afterwards, it will be seen what strange fish the flood brings in with it.

Callinicos on Althusser

> The identification of which I spoke in introducing (the Hegelian Marxists') work – of the problem of the unity of theory and practice and the problem of the relation between science and its object is an invalid and illicit conflation of questions of quite a different order. The first problem is the fundamental problem of Marxist politics: how to give ideas a material force. . . . The second problem is an epistemological one: how to guarantee that a theory does in fact produce a knowledge of the reality it claims to explain. (Alex Callinicos, *Althusser's Marxism*, pp. 22–3).

It is one of Althusser's great merits to have definitively

cleared up this confusion, and Callinicos gives him some credit for this.

However much it may be necessary to criticize Althusser's earlier 'theoreticism' (and it *is* necessary), it must not be at the expense of returning to this historicist confusion[2] which, aiming to solve two problems at once, actually impedes the solution of either. It appears to solve both problems, because it treats theory as one necessary aspect of social practice arising more or less spontaneously out of that practice and reflecting it more or less accurately. Theory and practice are said to be 'inseparable' – any practice has its theoretical aspect, any thoery is an aspect of some practice. This essential unity is seen as guaranteeing both the practical effectiveness of the theory, and its legitimacy as a theory *about* the social practice of which it is an aspect.

But if theory and practice are originally 'inseparable', the very real political problem of how to *unite* them cannot arise; hence the pertinence of Lenin's phrase – the *fusion* of theory and practice. It emphasizes that this union is a practical task not a theoretical given.

It need not be denied that there *is* a theoretical aspect to any practice, or that theory itself is the work of a practice, and indeed Althusser asserts both things. But what must be rejected if one is to make sense of revolutionary politics is the idea that the spontaneous 'theory' or theorization arising out of a given practice is necessarily *true of* that practice. It may be necessary to challenge the spontaneous theorization with a scientific theory, in order to transform the practice from a mystified to a clearsighted one.[3]

This leads to the other problem – the epistemological one. Knowledge has to be sought out; it does not reveal itself mystically to the adept of practice. The idea that it does is very prevalent on the left, but has an extremely suspect genealogy. One need only look at the use of this idea in military and bureaucratic ideology, to prevent political questions being asked about military and bureaucratic practices ('that is all theory, we are the practical men, we know what is best' and so on). By rejecting any theory but that which is intrinsic to the practice concerned, all criticisms of existing practices are repressed.

Althusser's insistence that not only true but also false ideas come from social practice, and his demonstration of the need to distinguish different practices with different epistemological statuses, have made adherence to the inseparability thesis inexcusable. Yet in the end, Callinicos has two main criticisms of Althusser: that, despite having provided the grounds for abolishing epistemology altogether, he continues to use epistemological concepts; and that he evades the problem of the unity of theory and practice. The conjunction of these two criticisms makes me wonder whether Callinicos is unwittingly appealing to the attractiveness of the above historicist confusion for many Marxists. If this is not so, then it is difficult to see what is meant by the second criticism.

True, Althusser's notion of theory as theoretical practice abolishes the problem of the relation of theory-in-general to practice-in-general, for theoretical production is itself a practice. But it does so as part of a theory of a hierarchy of relatively autonomous practices – economic, political, ideological, theoretical etc. So that the political problem is not abolished but reformulated: how to secure the transformation of the 'political' practice of class struggle from an economistic and reformist one (which it will spontaneously tend to be), into one which raises the issue of state power, by uniting Marxist theory with that practice. There are no great theoretical problems about this – Lenin's *What is to be Done?* already solves most of those that exist. There is the immense *practical* problem of carrying out this union and transformation. But the theoretical problems encountered in this practice are different ones, concerning the nature of ideology, and of the specific ideological formations present in the dominated classes of advanced capitalist societies. These are problems for historical materialism, not for philosophy.

What then is Althusser being criticized for? At one point, Callinicos even quotes with apparent approval Regis Debray's sneer: 'Theory draws its effectiveness from its rigorousness, and its rigorousness is effective because it separates "development in reality" from "development in thought", "the operation of society" from the "operation of knowledge." In other words, all we had to do to become good theoreticians was to be lazy bastards' (quoted *op. cit.*, p. 60). The only *thought* that I can discern behind this numbing non-sequitur is the idea that theory springs fully armed from the head of political practice – that is a denial of the hierarchy of practices and a reversion to the historicist conflation of political and epistemological problems referred to at the beginning. For if theory does not automatically arise from non-theoretical practice in this way, then hard theoretical work needs to be done in order to produce it. And Debray, like many others of the left, is no doubt unable to see theoretical work as other than 'laziness', time taken off from political work.

But there are other problems for Callinicos if he wants to hold to the distinction made at the beginning. For his first criticism of Althusser implies that epistemological problems are false problems anyway. And if there is no epistemological problem, it cannot be conflated with anything. We must return to the question of epistemology, and ask whether the obituary Callinicos and many others are writing on it is not premature.

Let me say first that as I understand Althusser (and leaving aside some unfortunate passages in *Essays in Self-Criticism*), he neither wishes to abolish epistemology, nor provides grounds for its abolition. Indeed his whole anti-historicist achievement takes place within epistemology, and stands or falls with it.

There are three aspects of Althusser's thought which give rise to Callinicos's claim that he has undermined epistemology. The third of these appears only in his later work, and is treated separately by Callinicos, so I shall leave it aside for the moment. The first is the assertion that, as each science provides its own procedures of validation, there is no general criterion of scientificity. This is true if it is interpreted correctly. The procedures of validation in say mathematics, chemistry, evolutionary biology and linguistics could hardly be more dissimilar. Is this the abolition of epistemology? If so, the credit goes not to Althusser but to Kant:

> If truth consists in the agreement of knowledge with its object, that object must thereby be distinguished from other objects; ... Now a general criterion of truth would be such as would be valid in

each and every instance of knowledge, however their objects may vary. It is obvious however that such a criterion cannot take account of the content of knowledge (relation to its object). But since truth concerns just this very content, it is quite impossible, and indeed absurd, to ask for a general test of the truth of such content. A sufficient and at the same time general criterion of truth cannot possibly be given. (*Critique of Pure Reason*, A 58–59, B 83).

But for Kant this rejection of a general epistemological *criterion* does not deny – indeed it assumes – that truth is correspondence of a theory with its object. The rejection of a single criterion of *truth* for use in all the sciences is not the same as the rejection of a criterion – based on the nature of truth as correspondence of thought with reality – by which science can be distinguished from pseudo-science. Of course one tests a hypothesis of linguistics in a totally different way from the way one tests a hypothesis of chemistry. In each case, the difference stems from a difference in subject-matter, and the need for each theory to be appropriate to its own subject-matter. But in each case one does interrogate the subject-matter in ways which are not arbitrary, but determined by the project of acquiring objective knowledge.

But to return to the Althusser of *Reading Capital*: the second aspect of his alleged 'abolition of epistemology' is that he substitutes the 'question of the *mechanism* of cognitive appropriation of the real object by means of the object of knowledge, for the ideological question of *guarantees* of the possibility of knowledge' (*Reading Capital*, p. 56, quoted by Callinicos, p. 58).

Callinicos interprets this as meaning that a causal account of the foundations of science replaces the general criterion of scientificity sought by 'epistemology'. But this causal account must be the work of a meta-theory – 'the theory of theoretical practice' (Althusser's definition of philosophy in his early writings).

There are all sorts of problems about this. Althusser was later to recognize some of them, but it is arguable that, in exorcizing one devil ('theoreticism'), he made room for seven devils to enter.

If the meta-theory is itself a science (the science of sciences), it either becomes a master-science, as rationalist philosophy aspired to be, or it would be an aspect of some existing science which accounts for the process of theoretical production as part of its own object. But either way one would then want to know what sort of knowledge it gave about scientific practices. If it were a causal account and nothing else, what would it show? It could show *how* particular sciences ensure their capacity to appropriate reality in knowledge. But in each case it must be that and not something else that they are doing. It is not enough to trace the causal mechanisms involved in the production or validation of a theory; it must be shown why those mechanisms are relevant ones, how they establish that the theory is true *of* a reality which is itself outside the theory and independent of it.

Furthermore the history of the sciences is part of history, and historical materialism is the science of history. If a causal account is all that is wanted, this science can provide it without the services of philosophy. And such a solution is just what is intimated by the cryptic note on p. 124 of Althusser's *Essays in Self-Criticism*[4]. But to regard the task of the validation of scientific knowledge as falling to historical materialism as the theory of history in general and therefore also of the history of the sciences, is to dive back into the murky pool of historicism—making the science of history the master-science, abolishing philosophy and with it the distinction between science and ideology. For considered as one social practice among others, science can indeed be legitimately studied as ideology, as located in the superstructure—where else? The ideological roots of the discoveries of Newton or Darwin or Marx or Freud can be laid bare without invalidating those discoveries. The science/ideology distinction is an epistemological one, not a social one.[5]

It is impossible to think the relation of science to other social practices by means of the concept of relative autonomy. Considered as one social practice among others, with miscellaneous economic, political and ideological relations to other social practices, science has no special autonomous status. Considered as the appropriation of the real in objective knowledge however, it is radically and categorically autonomous. For as such it is defined by its norm of correspondence to the real, and in so far as it achieves this norm, it succeeds, whatever its genealogy. Insofar as we want to know about the reality of which a science speaks, the social, psychological and linguistic accidents concerning the practice of that science are simply of no interest, any more than the colour of the scientists' hair. It is therefore as true and as misleading to say that a science is also an ideology as to say that a human being is a pile of chemicals or that Beethoven's Ninth Symphony is a succession of noises. And indeed, as false, remembering that the same human individual will be at different times composed of different molecules, and that many successions of noises have been performances of Beethoven's Ninth. Scientific knowledge does not change its nature when the writings embodying it are translated from German into English, or when it is applied in the service of the proletariat rather than the bourgeoisie, or when the experiments that test it are performed in Peking instead of New York. The reduction of science to ideology is not a misidentification of a social institution, it is a category mistake.

But that is not the end of this shocking affair, for if historical materialism were granted the right to pass judgement on the sciences by virtue of the fact that they fall within its object as social practices, the other sciences could claim equal credentials for the role of master-science. Psychology, because the thinking of scientists, like any other mental process, is subject to its laws: linguistics, because scientific discourse is produced in accordance with the rules of language; logic, whose laws it must obey if it is to be coherent thought; evolutionary biology, for the capacity for scientific discovery is an adaptive species-specific trait of human beings; and to reduce the whole thing to its absurdity, physics, because scientists, laboratories, textbooks etc. are after all composed of atoms.

The need to be on guard against the usurpation of epistemological functions by the particular sciences, does not mean that we cannot use particular sciences in the course of epistemological enquiries into other sciences. But the question of the legitimacy of such inter-theoretical interventions is itself an epistemological question.[6] That they are often illegitimate should be obvious to anyone who reflects on the history of those theoretical ideologies denoted by

adding the suffix 'ism' to the name of the theoretical aggressor:
psychologism, historicism, biologism, physicalism, and
perhaps rationalism (taking 'reason' to refer to logic and
mathematics).

So the task of drawing the line between science and non-
science still falls to a philosophical discipline – epistemology.
Which brings us back to the question: just what is it that
Althusser wants to substitute for the question of guarantees?
In the first place, it is quite certain that he did not in his
earlier writings fall victim to any of the false solutions I have
been discussing. 'When we pose the question of the *mechanism*
by which the *object* of knowledge produces the cognitive
appropriation of the *real object*, we are posing a quite different
question from that of the conditions of the *production* of
knowledge'. (*Reading Capital*, p. 61). The history of the
production of knowledges fails to reflect 'the fact that these
products are not just any products, but precisely knowledges'
(p. 62). Althusser is still asking the philosophical question with
which he started: 'to read *Capital* as philosophers is precisely
to question the specific object of a specific discourse, and the
specific relationship between this discourse and its object; it
is therefore to put to the *discourse-object* unity the question of
the epistemological status which distinguishes this particular
unity from other forms of discourse-object unity.' (*Reading
Capital*, p. 15) The term 'mechanism' does not allude to a
promised causal analysis of the foundations of science, but
to an aspect of theoretical production which explains the
relation of its product to the world, that is a relation of
'cognitive appropriation'.

Callinicos is quite right then to go on to say: 'the theory of
theoretical practice is a theory of the difference between
science and ideology. Since it is responsible for *establishing*
scientificity as such, the theory must involve a general
criterion of scientificity.' (*op. cit.* pp. 59–60) And this is
certainly epistemology. But why *bourgeois* epistemology, as
Callinicos claims? If it is alleged that all epistemology is
bourgeois, this needs to be shown. And if one rejects Bogdanov's ludicrous idea of bourgeois science and proletarian
science (with different contents), it is not obvious why one
should talk of bourgeois epistemology at all. Perhaps this

epithet could be applied to an epistemology which, like Popper's, was purpose-built to deny historical materialism's claim to scientificity, or which, like Feyerabend's rejection of epistemology (the only consistent such rejection), was purpose-built to provide scientific credentials to every theoretical ideology. But Althusser is not Popper or Feyerabend.

Yet an important point of interpretation does emerge from this criticism. Once one understands the sort of thing Althusser means by 'mechanism', that is, in particular, once one has distinguished it from a causal account provided by another science, the question of the mechanism of cognitive appropriation comes to look not unlike the question of guarantees, once *this* question is distinguished from the Cartesian quest for absolute certainty. By taking his stand on Marx's 1857 Introduction he has certainly moved beyond *classical* 'bourgeois' epistemology (from Descartes and Hobbes to Hegel and Mill). He has done so in that (1) he is asking: How is objective knowledge produced? not: How do individual subjects acquire knowledge? and (2) he does not confuse epistemological and ontological questions, and in particular, does not reduce the latter to the former. These two advances are not original to Althusser – they are present in Marx and Lenin, though Althusser has done good work in rescuing them from under the rubble of historicism where the Marxism of 1920 – 50 had buried them.

But neither are they specifically Marxist – they are shared ground with the schools of, for instance Popper and Bachelard. They do not distinguish 'bourgeois' from Marxist epistemology, or epistemology from no epistemology; they distinguish scientific realist epistemology – or, to use a term more familiar in the Marxist tradition, materialist epistemology – from empiricism and rationalism (both of which were more or less compromised by idealist features), and from frankly idealist philosophies which treated truth as having nothing to do with the relation of the theory to anything outside itself. The points of contact that the materialist epistemology of Marxist philosophers has with that of some bourgeois philosophers should not be a cause for concern. If Marxism can only retain its identity by taking positions utterly distinct from all bourgeois theories, then it is still parasitic on bourgeois thought (as its inversion). It is easy to bill the rejection of epistemology as a valiant Marxist break with the trendy bourgeois sages Bachelard and Popper. It is more correct to see it as the discarding of these outmoded fashions for the now trendy Derrida and Feyerabend.[7]

One last look at Callinicos on Althusser's earlier position (that is that of *For Marx* and *Reading Capital*, characterized by the definition of philosophy as the theory of theoretical practice). Callinicos tells us:

> To assert the autonomy of theoretical practice without establishing the specific character of the relation it enjoys with the social whole, is to transform the sciences into an instance above and cut off from the social process. This unquestionably is the result of an epistemology according to which the relation of theory to the other social practices rests purely on their common structure, and the preservation intact of this relation is the prerogative of philosophy whose only relation beyond itself is with the sciences. From the standpoint of Marxism, it is clearly a position that must be rejected. Otherwise, Marxism would become a theory lacking in any actuality beyond the theoretician's cabinet, any relation to the life and struggle of the proletariat (*op. cit.*, p. 77).

I have already said something about the first point. For scientific epistemology as 'epistemology without a knowing subject' as Popper has well expressed it, the question of the relation of science to other social realities (except as its objects) *cannot be raised*. It can be raised in other (socio-historical) contexts, but it has no epistemological interest.

Second, the common structure (that of production) which theory shares with other social practices, is not the only relation between theory and those practices, nor a particularly important one for epistemology. Insofar as the theory concerned is theory of society, its relation to those practices is one of knowledge. It is this and this only that makes theory of use to the workers in struggle. The use of theory in no way rests on its *source*: that would be to fall right back into the historicist conflation referred to at the beginning.

So the last sentence of the last quote in no way follows from what has gone before. The value of Marxist theory to the workers' movement is precisely that it gives objective knowledge of the society of which that movement is part, and on which it is trying to act in order to transform it into something different.

But if Althusser can be acquitted on the charge of precluding an adequate theory of the relation of theory to practice, and if his project of a scientific epistemology is a valid one, that does not mean that his own epistemology is fully adequate in *For Marx* and *Reading Capital*. It really does contain rationalist residues, both in the status granted to philosophy or epistemology (a little too much like the queen of the sciences, too little like their underlabourer), and in the content of the account of the epistemic 'mechanisms'. It is this last matter which is the really serious flaw in Althusser's epistemology, and the more serious as it is not overcome but compounded by many of his critics (Timpanaro being an exception).

For when Althusser comes to speak of the mechanism by which the process of knowledge appropriates the real object, he rejects genetic accounts of knowledge *without distinguishing them from experimental accounts*. He insists that one must consider the scientific theory, with its hierarchy of concepts and order of proofs, as a synchronic system, without asking about its origin. There is a sense in which this is correct, as is shown by the fact that it is possible to study a science quite adequately without studying its history. And in general it is a sound principle that one needs to know what something is before one can investigate how it came to be what it is; and that it is a mistake to try to determine the nature of something by referring to its past history (see 'degenerated workers' states').

But experiments are a different matter. They are not necessarily the means by which scientific theories originate, but they are the means by which they are tested. But it is essential to the notion of an experiment that it be so constructed that the result is causally dependent on the nature of the real object. This is what is meant by calling an experiment 'a question put to nature'. There is no 'empiricism' here – it is not assumed that *within knowledge* there is a privileged stratum of *protokolsätze*.

The idea of putting questions to nature does not presuppose that nature has her own language in which to answer, independent of our theories. Much of the anti-epistemological case rests on the unargued assumption that it does. For instance:

> If testing is a rational procedure then there must be an a-theoretical mode of observation governed by a pre-established harmony between language and the real. To maintain, as Popper does, both the rationality of testing and the thesis that observation is an interpretation in the light of a theory is to collapse into a manifest and absurd contradiction. (Hindess, *Philosophy and Methodology in the Social Sciences*, p. 186).

This passage, I take it, is meant to be a complete argument, not just a step in one. It is supposed to be *manifestly* incoherent both to recognize that there are no theory-independent observation-statements, and at the same time to test the theory by reference to observations (experiments). This would only be true if the theory determined, not only the nature of the experiment and the way the result is interpreted, but the result itself. Yet it is of the essence of an experiment that it has more than one possible outcome, and that it depends on nature, not on the theory, which outcome occurs. There is nothing about this fact which requires that the outcome be described in theory-independent terms. Only that it be causally dependent on structure of reality, which is itself independent of the scientist and his or her theories.

But Althusser gives the distinct impression (in *Reading Capital*, p. 63) that *any* causal relation between the real object and our knowledge of it must be ruled out as 'geneticism'. Yet the knowledge that such and such an experiment produced such and such a result, and would do so again if repeated, belongs to the 'synchronic' structure of a science. No doubt Althusser does not deny this. But that is not good enough: for experiment is absolutely essential to scientificity, it *is* the mechanism of cognitive appropriation of reality.

In the absence of a full discussion of this crucial question, Althusser's statements about 'the systematicity of the system' producing the knowledge-effect (*ibid*, p. 68) can only give the impression of rationalist criteria (coherence, logical order) for knowledge. It is this residual rationalism, I would suggest, which leads Althusser to choose *mathematics* as his example when he is arguing for the internality to a theoretical practice of its criteria of validity. For although he goes on to say that in the 'experimental' sciences experiments are the criteria, he makes this sound as if it is an accidental feature of a certain number of sciences. In reality, it is to do with the nature of any knowledge of the real world (which of course does not include mathematics, but does include the 'human' sciences).

Callinicos, I feel, has misidentified the flaw in Althusser's earlier, 'theoreticist' position: it is not the neglect of *politics*, as Callinicos seems to think – it is the neglect of experiment. However when Callinicos has finished with Althusser's earlier epistemology, he lets him off the hook on account of his later work (*Lenin and Philosophy* and *Essays in Self-Criticism*). According to the new definition of philosophy in these works (with which I may say I am in broad agreement[8]), philosophy is not the 'theory of theoretical practice' that is a sort of master-science or metascience, but rather 'the class struggle in theory'. But this emphatically does not mean that philosophy should abandon its commitment to objectivity. On the contrary, if it is partisan, it is the partisan *of* 'the materialist thesis of objectivity'. To defend the sciences is to engage in class struggle in theory, because 'true ideas always serve the people; false ideas always serve the enemies of the people' *Lenin and Philosophy*, p. 24). Only the exploiting classes can gain from ideological error and ideological obstacles in the path of the sciences.

What place can epistemology have in such a philosophy? Well, the theoretical categories of philosophy have a practical function, which 'consists in "drawing a dividing line" inside the theoretical domain between ideas declared to be true and ideas declared to be false, between the scientific and the ideological' (*Lenin and Philosophy*, p. 61).

Callinicos's gloss on this is: 'Thus philosophy, far from being the instance which provides the sciences with the guarantee of their validity, becomes a practice, which, at best, can serve to defend already constituted sciences with their own, specific, internal criteria of validity, against the encroachments of ideology.' (*op. cit.*, p. 80) But this does not quite follow. Or at least, it begs the question, for what are 'already constituted sciences?' Ideologies do not always carry banners saying 'Down with science!' (though it is surprising how often they do). Many theoretical ideologies present themselves as sciences and make out a plausible case. Is one to defend marginalist economics or social ethology against what one see as the encroachments of (Marxist) ideology? When the minister preaches about sin, it can be taken for granted that he will be against it. Similarly when the Marxist speaks of ideology. But which are the sheep and which are the goats? If one is to draw a dividing line between theoretical ideologies and sciences, one needs criteria of scientificity. How does one know that historical materialism is scientific and astrology is ideological? Or, to take an issue on which Marxists are disagreed, how is one to determine whether behaviourism, psychoanalysis or humanistic psychology are scientific? They all have their own criteria for validating or rejecting hypotheses. But they cannot all be true.

There is one answer which could be given here: that our acceptance of historical materialism flows from a prior commitment to the proletarian class position. But this is to *abandon* the 'materialist thesis of objectivity', to substitute war cries for knowledge of how to shoot, to disarm the workers' movement theoretically. It was not for this that Marx slammed the door on Weitling.[9]

Callinicos rejects this answer, but he does not seem to recognize that in doing so he is rejecting the only interpretation of the thesis that philosophy in class struggle in theory which could make it appear as an alternative to epistemology.

> This thesis should not be seen as any sort of crude reduction of philosophy to politics. Rather, it is the assertion that the positions taken up in relation to the materialist theses, and in relation to the scientific or unscientific character of particular theories, is determined in the last instance by the interests of the different classes...
>
> ... one could argue that Karl Popper's attempt to demarcate science from pseudo-science, and to include historical materialism and psychoanalysis in the latter category, was determined in the last instance by the bourgeoisie's political need to deny these sciences any objective validity, since they presented a massive threat to bourgeois ideology. (*Althusser's Marxism*, p. 81)

No doubt this is true, but that does not give any grounds for the validation of one particular theory. If Popper regards historical materialism and psychoanalysis as pseudo-sciences because he is a bourgeois and full of defence-mechanisms, and I regard them as sciences because I am a malcontent and a degenerate, and *if that is all that there is to be said*, then Popper is at least wrong about one belief which he shares with Marx, Lenin, Althusser, Callinicos and myself: 'the materialist thesis of objectivity'. But if there *is* something more to be said, that something will be epistemological. It is then imperative for Marxists to enter battle with Popper, not merely on the ground of his class ideology, but either on the ground of his interpretation of the theories in question, or on the ground of epistemology.

I am not denying that class standpoints can have helpful as well as distorting effects, or that Marx could not have made his epistemological break had he not taken up a proletarian class position, from which realities were visible that were hidden to bourgeois ideologists. But recognition of this cannot replace epistemology: either there remain objective criteria for establishing the scientificity of Marx's theory, or one decides on political grounds. If the latter, one still has an epistemology, but an idealist (pragmatist, relativist) one.

Callinicos, as a good Marxist, has too much of a 'robust sense of reality' to draw idealist conclusions from his rejection of epistemology. But idealism is the only direction in which this can lead and, in the next text I shall consider, it gets there.

The Road to Kaliningrad

Lenin criticizes Kant's subjectivism in the name of a materialist thesis which is a thesis conjointly of (material) existence and of (scientific) objectivity. (Althusser, *Lenin and Philosophy*, p. 114)

There is no question here of whether *objects of discourse* exist independently of the discourses which specify them. Objects of discourse do not exist at all in that sense: they are constituted in and through the discourses which refer to them. The distinction/

correlation structure of epistemology depends on the conception of objects existing independently of knowledge yet in forms appropriate to knowledge itself. To deny that conception is to reject epistemology and the field of problems defined within it. (Cutler, Hindess, Hirst and Hussain *Marx's Capital and Capitalism Today*, pp. 216–17).

Marx's Capital and Capitalism Today is a book by four Marxists which rejects almost every main Marxist idea: the theory of value, exploitation (in the classical Marxist sense), laws of tendency, the possibility of correspondence or non-correspondence between forces and relations of production (the central dialectical discovery of Marx), modes of production, structural causality, the determinance in the last instance of the economic structure; politics as class struggle, the distinction between reform and revolution, and (though in a rather tongue-in-cheek sense) the possibility of a classless society.

As far as I can tell, the only survivors of this epistemological holocaust are: classes, defined by the relation of possession or separation between the economic agents and the means of production; and the methodological principle of rejecting explanations of historical processes in terms of the will and consciousness of agents. These survivors are certainly crucial parts of Marxist theory, but hardly peculiar to it, and not conjointly sufficient to distinguish Marxist practices – either theoretical or political from many others.

Such a drastic revision ought not to be ruled out *a priori*. It would, I believe, be more accurate to call it an abandonment of Marxism rather than a revision of it, but it would be dogmatic to refuse to consider this possibility. If Marxism will not stand up to scrutiny, or does not give the best available account of the workings of society, it should be rejected. Such rejection would not necessarily lead to the abandonment of socialist politics, any more than the replacement of Newtonian science by Einsteinian undermined technology – on the contrary, it made new practices possible within it. It cannot be ruled out in principle that Marxism will be replaced by a superior scientific theory on which an improved strategy for the workers' movement could be based.

But it seems to me that the common element of their critique of these diverse concepts is the idea that classical

Marxism is essentialist; this essentialism is seen as flowing from a rationalist epistemology; and this epistemology is rejected, not in favour of Humeian empiricism (the only alternative epistemology of which they seem able to conceive) but in favour of no epistemology at all.[10]

I will argue that classical Marxism is not essentialist, rationalist or indeed empiricist, but represents a genuine breakthrough to a materialist epistemology, and that the rejection of epistemology leads these authors to a rather extreme form of idealism.

The argument is set out as follows: first, I will try to show that their essentialist interpretation of some central Marxian concepts is a misinterpretation, stemming from a dogmatic refusal to understand what is original in Marx, a reduction of his innovations to pre-Marxian categories. Second, I will propose an interpretation of Marx's epistemology which shows that it is not reducible to classical rationalist or empiricist notions, and does not have any tendency to produce these essentialist errors. Third, I will look at the 'non-epistemology' espoused by these four authors, and draw out its similarities with Kant. I shall make some suggestions for a materialist resolution of the problems which give rise both to Kant's epistemology and post-Althusserian echoes of it. I shall conclude this section by focussing again on the content of Marx's theory, contrasting it both with the misreading of it perpetrated in *Marx's Capital and Capitalism Today*, and with the alternative type of theory presented in that book.

Interpreting Marxian Concepts
First, I want to look at their criticisms of some specific Marxist concepts.

The labour theory of value
The point of this theory is not, I take it, primarily to explain the prices of commodities, but to give an account of the necessity for a proportionate distribution of social labour, and the various mechanisms, specific to various modes of production, by which equilibrium in this distribution can be restored. I shall therefore proceed straight to their criticisms of this aspect of the theory.

It is just the concept of equilibrium that they dislike most, both in the work of Rudolf Hilferding and in that of I.I.Rubin. There is something of an attitude of 'heads I win, tails you lose' in their treatment of the respective arguments of these two Marxist political economists; also a sort of conceptual witch-hunting technique of guilt-by-association.

The concept 'equilibrium', it seems, has suckled two devils: economism and teleology.

> In the concept of 'equilibrium' we see the economistic hope of an end to capitalist relations of production. 'Equilibrium', the state of capitalism's vitality, is also the threat of its death.
>
> Should equilibrium conditions be threatened, systematic non-reproduction is possible, a systematic non-reproduction which undermines the relations of production. This fantasy is the dark side of a functionalism – the death that awaits the organism if its vital mechanisms are inhibited. (*ibid*, p. 71)

I would hate to see this style of argument generalized. Consider the following:

> Fred: Man must eat before he can think.
> Joe: You are a Heideggerian! I shall prove it!
>   He who speaks of the necessity of eating, admits the possibility of starving to death. Hence your whole philosophy is based on anxiety in the face of death. Ergo: You are a Heideggerian. QED. Take him away and cut his concepts off!

But people who talk of equilibrium generally believe that it can indeed be disturbed (what is happening to the economy now, comrades?), but also that a new equilibrium can often be established. They are in no way committed to the idea of a 'terminal crisis'. And even if they were, they would not be committed to the idea that such a crisis would lead to the supersession of capitalism without political struggle, as is insinuated later in the same passage (see Norman Geras's excellent exposition of Luxemburg's theory of the collapse of capitalism and the historical alternatives of socialism or barbarism, in his book *The Legacy of Rosa Luxemburg*).

But the idea that there are mechanisms for the re-establishment of equilibrium is treated as equally flawed – this time because it is 'teleological-functionalist'. In their discussion of Rubin, they tell us: 'this variant of the Marxist theory posits a functionalism (a certain composition is necessary in an economy, this composition regulates production) and then makes *any* working economy exhibit this functionality (it must have a composition structure since production *must* be regulated – these goods would not be bought if they were not use-values). (*ibid*, p.87) 'What these gentlemen lack is dialectics'. The only concept of a totality of which they seem capable of conceiving, is of one which excludes dysfunctional aspects, which, in short, cannot generate contradictions. Either teleology is in its heaven and all is well with the economy, or there can be no self-regulating mechanisms, and every crisis is terminal. Yet the Marxist dialectic is nothing if not a theory of structures which reproduce themselves without teleology, and generate dysfunctions which can be contained but not eliminated within the structure.[11]

My accusation is not the dogmatic one of infidelity to Marx, but that they fail even to consider a central Marxian theoretical innovation as a possibility. It seems to be necessary to remind these epigoni of *Theoretical Practice* that there is such a thing as a 'de-centred structure-in-dominance'.

Motors of history and 'Subjects of History'

This treatment of equilibrium-theory as theory of economic systems as expressive totalities (for that is what is going on) is an instance of a more general tendency to read Marx in essentialist terms, and reject his theories about society on the ground that their alleged essentialist premises must be rejected.

Thus the 'laws of tendency' of capitalism and the succession of modes of production are seen as instances of an essential tendency of mankind to progress, to develop its productive forces; this is traced to a 'trans-historical subject' and myths of the self-production of man etc. Culter *et al.* quite rightly feel that there is no longer any need to argue against these myths, and that doctrines which stand or fall with them – must fall. But they fail to show that Marx does start from these premises. Capitalism develops the forces of production because of a dynamic internal to its structure, not because it is one avatar of an inherently self-developing Eternal Man.

There are in each case specific reasons why particular modes of production generate the forces which make possible transition to particular other modes of production – for example feudalism to capitalism or capitalism to socialism. It was only when, in *The German Ideology*, they decisively – not to say contemptuously – turned their backs on self-producing subjects etc., that Marx and Engels were able to formulate the materialist conception of history as a research programme.

The *a priori* determination of Culter *et al.* to find essentialism in Marx perhaps stems from a tendency to push the epistemological break further and further forward until it postdates the deaths of Marx, Engels and probably Lenin, and perhaps shifts out of history altogether, into eschatology. Of course, they do not deny that there are places in Marx's writings where he says things incompatible with essentialism and the consequent unilinear conception of progress in history, and it is this side of his thought that they wish to develop. But in interpreting his central concepts, they impute essentialism on the slenderest evidence.

Perhaps the most serious political consequence of this approach is the rejection of the analysis of politics in terms of class struggle, for if such analysis is misconceived it is difficult to see how Marxism is an advance over utopian socialism. They seem to be claiming that political movements could represent classes only as expressions of the will of those classes, not as complex effects of economic class struggle. It is a repetition of a mistake which has arisen before in connection with the Marxist theory of the state. Marx and Engels had (in the *Communist Manifesto*) said of *certain* states – namely the constitutional states based on limited suffrage which existed in the most advanced countries at the time of writing – that 'The executive of the modern state is but a committee for managing the common affairs of the whole bourgeoisie'. Some have taken this as a general theory of states as purpose-built instruments in the collective hands of the ruling class, but it is not so. Marx's analysis of France under the second empire, or of Germany under the Prussian monarchy, show the possibility of forms of state which, while they are effects of the class structure and the struggles it generates, and while they necessarily serve to perpetuate the economic power of the possessing classes, are not related to the ruling class in this way.

The relation of parties to class struggle is similar. The British Labour Party, for instance, does not represent the will of any class. It tries to resolve economic class struggle in a particular manner, determined by the effects of various economic class forces upon it (through its need to retain its trade-union base, appease petty bourgeois 'public opinion' for electoral reasons, co-operate with monopoly capital in the management of the economy, etc.). In doing so, it serves the needs of the bourgeoisie in preserving capitalism.

It is not, then, always possible to map parties onto the classes they represent, but this does not mean one has to see them as a plurality of pressure-groups with no closer connection to the class struggle than the anti-vivisection society. The assumption that it does stems from a wrong posing of the problem. It is posed in terms of the unity of classes at the economic, political and ideological levels. But such unity does not necessarily exist – Marxism has never claimed that it did. It is normally only in revolutionary situations that economic classes close their ranks and act as collective historical agents. But economic struggle goes on all the time.

Classical Marxism[12] certainly defines classes in economic terms (*pace* Poulantzas), but it was never asserted that classes so defined would necessarily cohere at the political and ideological levels. Rather, the organization of the working class as a political unity was to be the result of a protracted ideological struggle, by which the economic struggle which *is* given as a spontaneous effect of capitalist class-relations would be transformed into a struggle with revolutionary political objectives.

But for Cutler *et al.* this original discrepancy between economic and political class organization is a theoretical problem rather than a practical one. Either it is a matter of a discrepancy between objective interest and subjective consciousness of that interest, or the failure to develop a political class consciousness is itself an effect of the structure, determined in the last instance by the economy itself. In the first case, individual subjectivity is given an explanatory role, and no account is given of why other communal interest groups should not take precedence over class loyalities. In the second case, one is committed to a structural causality which, one is assured, is a version of expressive causality – that is essentialist.

Why the recognition of the discrepancy between class interest and political class consciousness should lead to 'subjectivism' one is not told. Could it not be explained by an objective but non-economistic theory of ideology? Perhaps, granted such a theory, one is back on the ground of Althusserian structural causality; but then what is essentialist about such a position? One is told it is functionalist – ideology is produced because the reproduction of the economic structure requires it. This may be a valid criticism of Althusser's paper on 'Ideology and the State' (in *Lenin and Philosophy*) of which I have argued elsewhere that it depicts the production of ideology as 'a conspiracy without a subject'. But such functionalism is not a necessary consequence of any scientific account of ideology. It is possible to recognize that capitalism produces dysfunctional ideological formations (for example Marsixm) and that the production of ideas in bourgeois society is as chaotic and unplanned as is material production, without leaving anything to subjective arbitrariness. Certainly ideology does, overall, serve to make possible the reproduction of capitalist class-relations – insofar as it does not, there is ideological crisis. But the evolution of ideologies is Darwinian, not Lamarckian.

But all these attributions of some form of subjectivism to Marx or other Marxists (whether the 'subjects' involved are de-historicized individual subjects or a trans-historical Absolute Subject), are 'must have' arguments: Marx *must have* assumed this, that, or the other thing (which he would not have admitted to assuming). In such cases it is useful to ask whether there is some other explanation of his position – and there is.

Cutler *et al.* do not really consider the possibility of an objective, materialist theory of subjectivity, which neither ignores the fact of human subjectivity, nor treats it as an irreducible datum. Yet classical Marxism has always assumed the possibility of such a theory, and although there is much work to be done in this field, there is some reason to believe that Marxism, with a little help from its psychoanalytical friends, will be able to achieve this.

But this neglect is an instance of an approach on the part of these authors which makes all that is original in Marxism invisible to them – their interpretation of any structure, any interconnected whole, as an expressive totality, of the sort that Althusser identifies in Hegel and the Hegelian Marxists.

Expressive totalities and determination in the last instance

Pre-Marxian thought – with the possible exception of Spinoza – conceives of the ultimate structure of reality whether physical or social, in one of two ways: either as the mechanistic interaction of atoms, themselves unstructured; or as forming a whole or wholes in which the parts had no autonomy, their nature following from the nature of the whole. The former was the view of seventeenth- and eighteenth-century empiricism and materialism, the latter of Leibniz and Hegel, with Kant representing a mixed position. In order to conceive of social structures in a materialist way (which earlier materialism had failed to do),[13] it was necessary to reject both atomism and holism, both of which depended on the idea of irreducible subjects (individual or Absolute), and neither of which could allow for the possibility of really existing conflicts, internal to and generated by the structure, yet threatening to destroy it.

For Marx, a social formation is a structure which is not the mere expression of its 'idea'; which has no centre, no purpose, no directing agency; which determines the social nature of its elements, *and* the contradictions between them. Its elements double as material beings subject to the laws of their own material nature, and as terms of social relations in which they occupy definite roles generated by the structure. There are various interlocking sub-structures whose nature cannot be read off from the overall structure.

Marx's achievement in theorizing this type of structure is marked by Althusser's concept of a 'de-centred structure-in-dominance', as contrasted with the 'expressive totality' of the idealists. Althusser points out that the metaphor of 'inverting' Hegel is inadequate. A society is not a mere expression of its economic structure, as according to Hegel it is an expression of its 'Idea'. A too literal interpretation of the inversion of Hegel leads at once to mechanistic-economistic distortions of historical materialism, and the repetition of idealist philosophical positions.

All these points, I had thought, were bridges burnt behind us.[14]

But no! One is now assured that the only way to conceive of the effectivity of a structure on its elements is in terms of an expressive totality which constitutes them; and that the economic structure cannot be determinant in the last instance within the social structure, unless the superstructure is a mere epiphenomenon of it. Both concepts are therefore rejected.

At this point one might be forgiven for thinking that one is going to be treated to a 'materialist' version of methodological individualism: come back Hobbes, all is forgiven.

Wrong again! One is told that this essentialism which they claim to detect in the notion of structural causality springs from a rationalist epistemology, and atomism from an empiricist epistemology. These are seen as the only alternative types of epistemology, and both wrong. It remains to be seen what alternative mode of seeing society springs from – no epistemology at all.

The argument is set out most clearly on pp. 213–14 of *Marx's Capital and Capitalism Today*:

> it should be noted that the different epistemological conceptions of the relation between discourse and its objects entail different conceptions of the relation between objects themselves.
>
> For empiricism, relations between objects . . . can only be conceived as given in experience itself. The classical empiricist conception of relations between objects is therefore in terms of a mechanical, external causality representing nothing more that the existence of regular and recurrent correlations between observed phenomena.
>
> In the rationalist epistemology, on the other hand, where the world is conceived as a rational order, concepts give the essence of the real and relations between concepts therefore represent the essential form of the relations between objects. The classical rationalist conception of relations between objects is therefore in terms of an

expressive causality, an internal relation between an essence and the phenomenal forms of its appearance. These relations between objects may be established through purely theoretical argument.

I shall not stop to dwell on the fact that there is a great deal of work in the field of scientific epistemology that is neither rationalist nor empiricist in these senses. Philosophy has not stood still since Leibniz and Hume. It is not only Marxists, either, who have transcended this alternative.

It is difficult to fit even Engels' statement that materialism means presenting the facts in their real and not an imagined connection, into this schema. The reference made in the same passage (*ibid*, p. 214) to 'the thesis of determination in the last instance, regarded by classical Marxism as beyond any merely empirical refutation' is astounding; if anyone can produce a single passage written by a 'classical Marxist' to substantiate this, I would be prepared to hang a portrait of Sir Karl Popper on my lavatory wall. But perhaps the best text to look at is Marx's 1857 Introduction, and ask of it: Is classical Marxism rationalist and essentialist? and, Are the only alternatives rationalism, empiricism or no epistemology at all? Short as this text is, it contains enough pointers to keep us clear of the main errors in the field of epistemology – I shall quote enough of it to make this evident, I hope.

One word of warning. It is thanks to Althusser and his followers that this text owes its justifiably high reputation in contemporary Marxist epistemology. But that should not lead us to read the whole of Althusser's epistemology into this text – he deserves some credit for his originality, but also for leading us up some original blind alleys.

Marx's Epistemology

(a) Thus, if I were to begin with the population, this would be a chaotic conception of the whole, and I would then, by means of further determination, move analytically towards ever more simple concepts, from the imagined concrete towards ever thinner abstractions until I had arrived at the simplest determinations. *From there the journey would have to be retraced until I had finally arrived at the population again, but this time not as the chaotic conception of a whole, but as a* rich totality of many determinations and relations. The former is the path historically followed by economics at the time of its origins.

(b) The latter is obviously the scientifically correct method. *The concrete is concrete because it is the concentration of many determinations*, hence unity of the diverse. It appears in the process of thinking, therefore, as a process of concentration, as a result, not as a point of departure, even though it

(c) *is the point of departure in reality and hence also the point of departure for observation and conception.* Along the first path the full conception was evaporated to yield an abstract determination; along the second, the abstract determinations

(d) lead towards a *reproduction of the concrete by way of thought.*

(e) In this way *Hegel fell into the illusion of conceiving the real as the product of thought......*

(f) Therefore, to the kind of consciousness – and *this is characteristic of the philosophical consciousness – for which conceptual thinking is the real human being, and for which the conceptual world as such is thus the only reality*, the movement of the categories appears as the real act of production – which only, unfortunately, receives a jolt from outside – whose product is the world; and – but this is again a tautology – this is correct in so far as the concrete totality is a totality of thoughts, concrete in thought, in fact a product of thinking and

(g) comprehending; but *not in any way a product of the concept which thinks and generates itself outside or above observation and conception; a product, rather, of the working up of observation and conception into concepts.*

(h) *The real subject retains its autonomous existence outside the head just as before; namely as long as the head's conduct is merely speculative, merely theoretical.* Hence, in the theoretical method, too, the subject, society, must always be kept in mind as the presupposition. (*Grundrisse* pp. 100–102. My emphasis throughout – A.C.).

From this we may gather the following:

(i) Knowledge is not a passive reflection of reality, impressed automatically on minds; it is a product of a human activity (a,d,g). Hence one is set on the road of a scientific epistemology, not an empiricist one.

(ii) This has misled the rationalists and idealists into thinking that, because science is our work, its *objects* are products of our minds (e,f). But it is not so; the real world exists prior to and independently of thought, and remains what it was after thought has replicated it (c,g,h). Thus, what

Bhaskar calls the intransitive object of science is recognized
(see below).

(iii) The aim of science remains to replicate just this
independent reality in thought, so it must constantly refer
back to the reality that it is trying to replicate (c,d,g,h). Thus
thought aims to correspond with its object, and is judged
according to its success in so doing.

(iv) In order to achieve adequacy to reality, science must
reconstruct the many-sided concreteness of that reality by
means of abstract concepts, brought into an interconnected
structure; and by means of such interconnectedness of these
concepts, there is reproduced in thought the complex inner
structuredness of the concrete reality of which that thought
is seeking to produce knowledge (a,b).

So that, if thought must deal in 'essences' by virtue of its
work of abstraction, it must bring together a complex multi-
plicity of these if it is to reproduce in thought the richness of
concrete reality.

(v) The abstractions of science reflect aspects of reality—
the 'many determinations' of which the concrete is the concentration (b). So these abstractions are not arbitrary, and their
appearance in the final product of science, the 'concrete in
thought', is not as impositions of ours, but as the concepts of
determinations discovered by us in reality (in so far that is, as
the thought really is adequate to its objects).

There is here, then, a sketch for an epistemology which has
radically broken with both rationalism and empiricism, and
which is thoroughly realist in its ontological assumptions and
experimental in its method—in short, which is scientific and
materialist.

It is clear that there is no tendency here to project onto
reality the relations between concepts. Rather, the relations
between concepts, though they may *seem* to be 'conceptual
relations', definitional, deductive and so on, are actually
attempts to match the relations between real 'determinations'
which conjointly constitute concrete reality. Thus, the
formulae of science, whether '$E = MC^2$' or the equations of
Capital, give knowledge of forces existing independently and
outside of thought.

In so far as they fail to match them, they have to be abandoned and new formulae constructed. The formulae may *seem* to be definitions but their terms acquire their meaning in the totality of the theory and practice of the science concerned, not merely from the formulae themselves.

Thus the 'method of presentation' may look as if it is essentialist, but the 'method of inquiry' is far from rationalist.

> Of course the method of presentation must differ in form from that of inquiry. The latter has to appropriate the material in detail, to analyze its different forms of development and to track down their inner connection. Only after this work has been done can the real movement be appropriately presented. If this is done successfully, if the life of the subject-matter is now reflected back in the ideas, then it may appear as if we have before us an *a priori* construction (Marx, *Capital*, I, p. 102).

This 'appearance' is common to all the sciences (see Bhaskar on the 'Leibnizian level' of science, in *A Realist Theory of Science*, pp. 173 – 4). The ontological assumption is not that real relations are structured like conceptual relations, but that relations between concepts can be made to map real relations.

At the same time it is clear that Marx does not share the conflation of epistemological and ontological questions which characterizes empiricism, at least from Berkeley on. This 'epistemic fallacy' as Bhaskar calls it, consists essentially in the idea that truth must have a subject, that for P to be true, there must be an answer to the question, who is to say that P? Bhaskar argues against this saying that it is necessary to distinguish what he calls the transitive object of science from its intransitive object. The intransitive object is the reality which science seeks to know, which pre-exists science and is unaffected by the knowledge science acquires of it; and which science never fully appropriates, but acquires ever deeper knowledge of. The transitive object is the real as known by the science of a particular time. It is never assumed to be the knowledge of the intransitive object. Progress in science is essentially progress towards an ever closer approximation to objective truth. Essentially, the intransitive object is Marx's 'real subject' (see (h), above), or Althusser's 'real object'. Lenin marks the same distinction by the terms relative and absolute truth (*Materialism and Empirio-Criticism*).

In this way the implicit assumption of an original complicity between subject and object, which characterized both rationalism and empiricism, is overcome. Yet it is not assumed that the intransitive object is unknowable, only that progress in the knowledge of it is a never-ending process of approximation. If science does not yield knowledge of the real, it loses its point.

Kant and Materialism

The authors of *Marx's Capital and Capitalism Today* however, have a different alternative to rationalism and empiricism, and an older one: 'far from providing an external measure for discourse, the entities referred to in discourse are constituted solely in and through the forms of discourse in which they are specified. Objects of discourse cannot be specified extra-discursively . . . ' (p. 216). One might as well say: one cannot talk about things without using words; therefore one cannot talk about things at all, only about words. Or again: knowledge consists of ideas; therefore one can only know ideas. Not a bad effort this, as the speculations of a youthful future bishop. But hardly clever for four learned post-Althusserians.[15]

Granted, there are two differences from Berkeley: ideas are conceived as linguistic realities, not as perceptual ones – this gives the whole thing a twentieth-century look. And it is not denied that there are things-in-themseves, only they would have to be unknowable. But such ideas also have been put forward before, and with a subtlety absent here – by Immanuel Kant. Compare the following by Cutler *et al*:

> Now we have argued that the epistemological project is not a necessary one and that the relations between discourse and its objects does not need to be conceived in terms of both a distinction and a correlation between a realm of discourse and an independently existing realm of objects. But in the absence of such an epistemological conception it is no longer possible to conceive of objects existing *outside* of discourse (and represented in its basic concepts) as the measure of validity of discourse. On the contrary, in the absence of such specifiable yet extra-discursive objects the elements specified in discourse must be conceived solely in and through the forms of discourse in which they are constituted. What is specified in theoreti-

cal discourse cannot be specified extra-discursively: it can be conceived only through that discourse or a related, critical, or complementary one. (*ibid*, pp. 228–229).

With the following by Kant:

> What then, is to be understood when we speak of an object corresponding to, and consequently also distinct from, our knowledge? It is easily seen that this object must be thought only as something in general = x, since outside our knowledge we could have nothing which we could set over against this knowledge as corresponding to it. (Kant, *Critique of Pure Reason*, A 104).

The difference is that Kant's thing-in-itself had the function of accounting for objectivity in appearance for an element of passivity on the part of the knower in relation to the known, for an 'empirical realism' within a 'transcendental idealism'. In short, Kant had 'a grain of materialism', which these authors have cast away.

And no wonder, for what they denounce as 'epistemology' – the thesis that a discourse and its objects are distinct, yet discourse should seek to correspond to its object – this thesis is precisely *materialist* epistemology[16]. The complicity of subject and object present in Descartes, Hume and others consists not in their idea that thought should correspond to its object, but in their failure to give adequate recognition to the distinctness of thought and object – that is not in their assertion of the second, but in their denial of the first postulate of materialist epistemology.

Althusser has criticized traditional epistemology for assuming this original complicity of subject and object – that is on the one hand the idea of (some) empiricists that the constituents of knowledge are also constituents of the known reality (Berkeley and his phenomenalist and neutral monist successors); and on the other hand the rationalist idea that there is a 'pre-established harmony' between the structure of mind and the structure of reality, enabling us to come to know reality deductively.

But it is strange indeed to see *scientific realist* or materialist epistemology accused of assuming such a complicity or pre-established harmony between thought and reality. For the whole point of scientific enquiry is to *establish* a harmony by *making* our thought conform to reality. A pre-established harmony would make the whole project of scientific experiment unnecessary. On the other hand a pre-established insulation of thought from reality, such as is postulated by Cutler *et al.*, would make science impossible.

Yet the question remains: if one is to take the materialist epistemological option, is one not assuming that reality is, at least, knowable by us? Why should reality be knowable? Someone once said to me, when I was arguing that the distinctions made by science reflect real distinctions: 'You seem to be assuming that there is Joe Reality somewhere out there, making sure that things turn out alright'.

Indeed it is bound to *look as if* there is such a Being; because an unknowable universe – though there is nothing logically contradictory about such an idea – could not have given rise to beings who can achieve knowledge, and who depend for their survival on such knowledge. In an unknowable universe, there would be no knowing subjects to know that it was unknowable.

It is a useful exercise for an epistemologist to reflect on the manner in which Darwin's theory dealt a death-blow to the idea of teleology in nature. There *appears to be* an 'original complicity' between species and their environment – because where the two are ill-suited, the species die out. Nature will always produce the appearance of design if it produces the appearance of anything, because where it does not produce that appearance, there will be nothing for it to appear to. There is no necessity about the knowability of nature, anymore than about the existence of Descartes; but whenever Descartes thought he existed, he existed sure enough. And anyone who asks: Is the universe knowable? lives in a knowable universe alright.

If one returns to Kant armed with these Darwinian insights, one can discard the transcendental idealist shell, and extract a very valuable kernel:

experience is itself a species of knowledge which involves understanding: and understanding has rules which I must presuppose as being in me prior to objects being given to me, and therefore as being *a priori*. They find expression in *a priori* concepts to which all objects of experience necessarily conform, and with which they must agree. (*Critique of Pure Reason*, B xvii-xviii).

Of course, we know that Kant thought that the understanding actively *imposed* its categories on the manifold of intuition, so that the 'must' at the end of the passage means: 'We have ways of making objects conform to our knowledge!' But one could make creative use of its ambiguity, and say: in order for empirical knowledge to be possible, reality must be structured in a certain way; and knowledge is possible, as the achievements of the sciences have shown; so reality *must* have that structure, objects *must* conform to our knowledge (in the sense that one says: 'It must have rained in the night', when one finds the kitchen floor flooded in the morning).

In this way, one could really have access to 'synthetic *a priori*' knowledge – not *a priori* in the absolute sense, but as the limiting case of the relative sense referred to by Kant (*ibid*, B 2). As knowledge, that is of the conditions of the possibility of knowledge – conditions which are only contingently realized, but the reality of which follows necessarily from the fact that there is such a thing as science. Some of these conditions may indeed be Kantian ones – spatio-temporal ordering, causality, countability, a principle of conservation and continuity and so on.

As Kant says of the reproducibility of representations in imagination (which is a condition of the possibility of knowledge):

> this law of reproduction presupposes that appearances are themselves actually subject to such a rule, and that in the manifold of these representations a co-existence or sequence takes place in conformity with certain rules. Otherwise our empirical imagination would never find opportunity for exercise appropriate to its powers, and so would remain concealed within the mind as a dead and to us unknown faculty. If cinnabar were sometimes red, sometimes black, sometimes light, sometimes heavy, if a man changed sometimes into this and sometimes into that animal form, if the country on the longest day were sometimes covered with fruit, sometimes with ice and snow, my empirical imagination would never find opportunity when representing red colour to bring to mind heavy cinnabar. (*Critique of Pure Reason*, A 100–101).

If our faculties of knowledge depend for their possibility on the structure of the world outside them in this way, why should one not assume that the world really has that structure and hence makes them possible, rather than that they have the additional, magic ability to force the world into a knowable form which it does not have in itself?

Such a materialist inversion of Kant would, I suggest, be far more fruitful for epistemology than all the somersaults and other circus tricks that Hegel has been compelled to perform posthumously by his Marxist ringmasters.[17]

Conceptual relations and the Materialist Dialectic.
But to return to Kant's post-Althusserian successors: one must now ask where their proposed final solution to the epistemological problem gets them. Does it rid them of the errors of rationalism? Does it enable them to think the relations between objects in a way that is neither essentialist nor mechanical? The answer to both questions, I fear, is no.

For what procedures are left to a theory in order to justify itself? Only its internal consistency, and its openness to criticism by another theory. But how does one decide between two internally consistent but conflicting theories? But their explanatory power? But what do they explain? Not 'the facts', that is for sure. A number of logically irrelevant criteria present themselves: political, aesthetic, humanistic. A consistent rejection of epistemology could not stop these being appealed to, anymore that it could stop complete arbitrariness. The motto would be Feyerabend's: anything goes! Our present authors want to let the sheep out of the fold and Feyerabend wants to let the wolves in, but the effect is the same.

No doubt these authors would differ from Feyerabend in demanding at least high intellectual standards, logical rigour etc. This brings them closer to traditional rationalism, but they are certainly at no advantage with respect to it. Everything happens in thought; theory is not only composed of concepts, it is about concepts; and if they can claim one up on rationalism for not imagining that reality itself is constructed deductively, by the same token they are in a worse state when it comes to the practical value of theory, for their theory has *no* relation with extra-theoretical reality.

Theories are useful when they say something about the world; *then* they can help us to act on it more effectively. It is all very well to clarify the relation between the concept of the possessing class and the concept of the state apparatus, but the concept of a boss cannot sack you and the concept of the fuzz cannot bust you.

They argue (*op. cit.*, pp. 219–20) that rationalism misled Marxists into regarding the superstructure as derivable in essence from the base, while in empiricism the relations of base and superstructure are held to lie 'beyond the range of theoretical determination'. According to their own view, all that can be said about the relation of base to superstructure is that each economic structure requires as a necessary condition of maintaining its existence, a superstructure from a definite range of possibilities. The necessity involved can hardly be causal or nomological necessity, for it is precisely the attempt to establish the reality of such necessities that they condemn in empiricism. Neither can it be some sort of 'conceptual' necessity which nevertheless exists in the real world, for belief in these is the error of rationalism. And if their avoidance of these two alternatives is made possible by their denial of any relation between thought and reality, one can only assume that they are left with a theory about the relations between the concept 'base' and the concept 'super-structure'—moreover a theory which scrupulously avoids saying anything about the relations between base and super-structure.

But in this case they get stuck on *both* horns of the dilemma: their theory deals only in concepts, so what can it do but 'derive essences'—not indeed in any attempt to extend our knowledge of reality thereby, but as a glass bead game of definitions and deductions. And as for the reality to which the theory *does not* refer, how can its elements be related except accidentally? What could the struggles of, say, the rising bourgeoisie against feudal superstructural institutions, have to do with that class's interest in the development of capitalism, and the obstacle to such development which those institutions constituted? Did the political struggles of this class *just happen* to promote its economic interests?

Surely one can discern real causal relations in history in such cases, without any recourse to essentialism.

I have been arguing that there is no reason in the epistemology or methodology of classical Marxism, why its content should be essentialist, holistic or teleological. I have also claimed that it does not in fact fall into any of these errors. Anti-Marxists who level these charges at Marx tend to regard it as uncontentious that he held these doctrines, and devote their energy to showing these position to be incorrect. Popper's anti-Marxist writing is like the Maginot line, a magnificent defence against Marxist theory, constructed along a frontier across which it was never the intention of Marxists to attack.

On the other hand Cutler *et al.* know perfectly well that the structures of which Marx or Althusser speak are not supposed to be essentialist 'expressive totalities', but they think that they cannot be anything else. Along with the inability to see an alternative epistemology to classical rationalism and empiricism, goes the inability to see the possibility of a type of structure which is distinct from a Hegelian totality or a Humean bundle. One has already seen the way they impose the alternatives 'functionalism/catastrophism' on theories of equilibrium. In *Pre-Capitalist Modes of Production*, Hindess and Hirst argue in a similar way that a believer in structural causality cannot work out a coherent theory of transition from one mode of production to another. In all these arguments, the possibility of a structure which is self-reproducing yet which generates internal contradictions is being denied, in a tone which implies that Marx must have overlooked the fact that that was what he was talking about. Yet what else is the content of the materialist dialectic?

So one must make clear what distinguishes the Marxian materialist conception of a structure and structural determination from the essentialist and atomist conceptions that it replaces. In the process I hope to remove doubts about the coherence of the Marxian conception.

In the first place, the structure has the property of maintaining itself in being while its elements change: hence it is not reducible to the sum of its elements; and at the same time, its self-reproduction is non-teleological – it does not depend on there anywhere existing a *purpose* of perpetuating the structure: hence it is unlike the holistic 'society as subject' which 'creates itself', which Marx and Engels ridiculed in *The German Ideology*.

Second, the structure assigns definite powers and limitations to its elements, which therefore cannot be understood atomistically; yet it does not *constitute* those elements, which also obey laws other than those of determination by the structure.

Third, a structure of this sort depends for its self-perpetuation on nature external to it. Thus, a society must find its raw material for production in its environment, and must satisfy the biological needs of its population, sufficiently to secure the physical survival and reproduction of its 'supports'. Every society exists under the constraint of geological and biological laws which it did not constitute.

Fourth, the structure may have irremediably imperfect mechanisms for securing its own reproduction; these mechanism are not for the most part systematically or 'deliberately' produced; and they are not only accidentally imperfect, that is they cannot in all cases be perfected within the structure, so that that structure could achieve 'immortality'.

In particular, class societies produce class antagonisms irreconcilable within those societies, which can (and to some extent always do) disrupt the society in question, and which may lead to its overthrow and supersession.

Social structures have no 'soul', no single principle or directing agency; but neither are they reducible to the interplay of many 'souls', the ideas and purposes of many individuals. 'Holism' and 'atomism' share the assumption that social explanation must be in terms of will or wills, conscious agency and purposes. In rejecting teleology, and every idealist or voluntarist form of explanation, a materialist theory of society, so far from falling midway between holism and atomism, clears itself of both at one stroke, and founds a theory of structural determination.

Marx demonstrates at length in *Capital* how capitalist firms, whose 'purpose' is to produce surplus-value (and this 'purpose' is itself determined by the structure), not only produce surplus-value but in doing so reproduce the material and structural conditions of existence of capitalism – new means of production, new workers, the same relation of separation between them.

The question how political and ideological formations are produced is more complex, but the solution is no more 'teleological'. The state and ideology are not for the most part *purpose-built* to secure the reproduction of capitalist relations. The policeman defends 'law and order' and in doing so defends the privileges of the bourgeoisie. The parson preaches spiritual values and in doing so offers sufferers an alternative solution to the relief of their suffering; he is not a conscious opium-pusher.

In order to achieve a materialist analysis of the super-structure, it is necessary to separate the question of the production of ideological and political institutions, from the question of the *role* of such institutions in the reproduction of class-relations. It is their failure to separate these questions, rather than any rationalist epistemology, which forces many Marxists into teleological explanations (for example the 'functionalism' of Althusser's essay on ideology and the state).

But if these questions are separate, how does it come about that the superstructure does in fact promote the reproduction of economic class-relations? Once again, the answer is not to be found in consciousness, teleology, providence, or Joe Reality; it is simply that if a hypothetical mode of production had no mechanism that secured this effect, that mode of production could not be instantiated. So that it is no accident that the only modes of production that exist are ones with mechanisms which do in fact do the job of creating the political and ideological conditions for their reproduction.

While on the subject of teleology, it is perhaps worth pointing out that biological organisms – so beloved of holistic/ teleological theorists as analogies ('society as an organism') – in fact are themselves materialist structures, governed not by a single constitutive principle, but by the complex, structured causal interaction of their elements with each other and with the outside world.

One who denies the possibility of materialist structures

invalidates not only materialist theories of society, but also materialist theories of biology. The break with atomistic behaviourism and essentialistic psychologies of consciousness achieved by psychoanalytic theory would likewise be called into question. If Spinoza and Marx are cast into the pit, it is with Darwin and Freud clutching their heels. And indeed, when Hindess criticizes Popper's use of Darwinian homologies in *Philosophy and Methodology in the Social Sciences*, he does accuse Popper of 'teleology' in a context which implies that Darwin was also guilty. The greatest victories over teleological explanation in the history of science are thereby tarred with the brush of teleology just because the phenomena they explain look teleological superficially. In this way, these authors situate themselves in pre-Darwinian as well as pre-Marxian theoretical space.[18]

This has taken us away from epistemology, but on the evidence of other texts by some of these four authors, it would seem that the rejection of essentialism may have motivated the rejection of epistemology. It is necessary to show that Marx is not guilty of essentialism or teleology in order to plead guilty to epistemology with a good conscience.

Requirements of an epistemology for the human sciences
Doubtless it will be asked: does not an epistemology which stresses the role of 'questions put to nature' (that is procedures so set up that the result depends on the structure of external reality), constitute just one more form of dogmatism? For if it is a definite enough criterion to exclude certain theoretical practices, must it not be claiming privileged access to reality for one form of enquiry?

This is easily answered. All that such an epistemology demands is that a theoretical practice *be* an enquiry into reality, that is, aims to measure its propositions against reality. Discourses which make no effort to conform themselves to reality can hardly object if a discourse which does attempt to do so claims superiority precisely in this respect: its correspondence to the real. Needless to say, epistemology does not rule out discourses which make no claim to yield objective knowledge—poetry, for instance. If simply insists that discourses that do make such claims try to fulfil them.

Experiment is simply the attempt to make the truth of ones conclusions *no accident*.

But it will be alleged that I am not arguing from the nature of science, but from the nature of truth; and that there is pre-scientific knowledge as well as a scientific one.

Naturally, it is true that one stumbles on 'facts' in everyday non-scientific practices, and that the element of truth in everyday conception of the world is also 'no accident' in that without some degree of knowledge, no practice would be possible. But – even without bringing in the fact that a Marxist theory of ideology shows that the error in this conception is no accident either – the testing of these conceptions within non-scientific practice is necessarily haphazard, being as it is no more than a by-product of the pursuit of practical needs. The whole value of science as separate, specialized activity[19], is that it lets the things themselves speak[20] instead of interpreting them in terms of our practical needs; that it so orders our practice (experiment) that its result depends on the structure of external reality, not on us. Science thus enables man to overcome the anthropocentricity which necessarily qualifies everyday knowledge based on practical experience. This in turn makes possible the development of radically new practices, which could never have been arrived at by mere practical experience. The immense progress achieved by the human race in the last three hundred years was made possible by this mutation which allowed science to emerge and liberate itself from immediate practical concerns. Of course this mutation had something to do with the rise of the bourgeoisie, but then the bourgeoisie of that era was carrying out an unprecedented development of human liberation. Reactionaries in radical clothes who wish to renege on the scientific achievements of the bourgeoisie should be recognized as partisans of the other historical alternative, of barbarism, not socialism.

For the rest, all that needs to be said about pre-scientific knowledge is that it is possible because everyday practice includes something analogous to experiment, though limited by its immediate practical purpose; to use the Freudian term, in includes reality-testing. Nevertheless, pre-scientific beliefs must give way to scientific ones when they clash.

Finally there is the question of the applicability or otherwise of the approach I have been defending to the human sciences. After all, Popper used a version of experimentalism to condemn Marxism and psychoanalysis. And with the exception of certain forms of psychological research (of rather doubtful value), experiment in the *laboratory* sense has little use in the human sciences. How does historical materialism, for instance, put its questions to nature (or to society)?

As a preliminary to answering this, it is useful to distinguish (using a passage from Husserl's *Logical Investigations*, I, pp. 230–1) between abstract or theoretical sciences, which 'are *nomological*, in so far as their unifying principle, as well as their essential aim of research, is a law', and concrete sciences, in which 'one connects all the truths whose content relates to *one and the same individual object, or to one and the same empirical genus*'. Husserl goes on to say that 'the abstract or nomological sciences are the genuine, basis sciences, from whose theoretical stock the concrete sciences must derive all that theoretical element by which they are made sciences'. No doubt this group (abstract sciences) includes physics, chemistry etc. As instances of concrete sciences, Husserl cites 'geography, history (that is presumably, historiography – A.C.), astronomy, natural history, anatomy etc'.

Now many of the characteristics of the concrete sciences are commonly ascribed to the social or human sciences. For instance, experiment as it exists in the abstract sciences is out of place in the concrete sciences listed above. The latter proceed by observation, description, and explanation in terms of abstract-scientific concepts, whereas the abstract sciences proceed by abstraction, deduction and experiment. Furthermore, prediction in the concrete sciences is always probabilistic (that is, what is likely to occur), and the falsification of predictions in them has no immediate theoretical consequences. The abstract sciences on the other hand make no predictions in the sense of forecasts, only conditional predictions (that is, what *will* occur given certain conditions). The foundation of Popper's shadow boxing with Marxism was his belief that Marxism was a concrete 'science' and nothing else. This belief is false, but not merely perverse; the relation between historical materialism as an abstract science and the concrete analysis of the concrete situation which Lenin called the heart of Marxism, is one which desperately needs clarifying. Embarrassment about the unclarified nature of this relation is no doubt one of the unconscious motives for the various forms of epistemological Luddism which are so prevalent on the left. For abstract sciences in general are tested independently of their use in various concrete sciences, by means of experiment. But in the case of Marxism, it is difficult to point to tests which are not in themselves applications. Where are the experiments? Here let me refer to Marx: 'in the analysis of economic forms neither microscopes nor chemical reagents are of assistance. The power of abstraction must replace both'. (*Capital*, I, p.90). However, in the natural sciences too, such abstraction has to be made before experiment becomes possible. The 'experimental conditions' of the laboratory are essentially reproductions in reality of abstractions that have already taken place in thought. The essence of 'laboratory conditions' is that irrelevant variables that would affect a process under natural conditions can be artificially eliminated. Any abstract science – natural or social – must abstract from aspects of the real of which it is not at that moment treating; but only in the natural sciences is it possible to actualize this abstraction and hence *measure* the real forces, in terms of the concepts of the science in question. For this reason, although the human sciences formulate concepts of forces, relations etc. which are in principle quantifiable (libido, the rate of exploitation and so on), they are not able to assign accurate numerical values to specific instances of these. Both historical materialism and psychoanalysis assume an ontology of quantifiable forces, without being able to quantify them (except as 'more' or 'less', 'high' or 'low', 'rising' or 'falling').[21]

This is not just a 'difference in method' between natural and human sciences – it is not *even* a difference in method. It is a disadvantage under which the human sciences labour, and which prevents them from achieving the same precision as the natural sciences. The persistent disagreements within Marxist or Freudian theory are only partly explained by the proneness of these sciences to the interventions of ideology (by virtue of their social implications). Their unavoidable imprecision is also at work here. And it is no use seeking humanistic consolations for this imprecision ('people are complicated, cannot be mathematically quantified, resist scientific analysis' etc. etc. etc.). These theoretical imprecisions lead to miscalculations in the practices based on them, which can have consequences far more tragic than any physicist's or pharmacologist's mistake has yet been (Stalin, Hitler).

Nevertheless, these imprecise sciences are better than no sciences at all. If they were not, one should forget about Marxism and revert to an empiricist practice of politics, in which there is no theory but 'learning by experience' – a sort of left Oakeshottism. Some Marxists would not be averse to this option, I think. It is implicit in Mandel's statement that it is by a 'historico-genetic method that we will succeed, rather than by an abstract attempt to work out concepts that risk being challenged by the next historical experiences. It is only the balance-sheet of history and revolutionary practice that will teach us to think more correctly'. (*New Left Review*, no. 100, p. 102). Concepts which do not *risk* being challenged by future historical experiences do not give any guidance about how to prepare for those experiences, and hence are useless for practice, while leaving theory to those with hindsight. If one needs theory at all, one cannot wait for the owl of Minerva.

'The proof of the pudding is in the eating' – very well, but if one has reason to suspect that the pudding is poisoned, one will be well advised to subject it to scientific tests before eating it. The *practical* advantage of theoretical science over practical experience is precisely this separation it makes possible between testing a theory and applying it.

Marxist science is not accurate enough to give us a fail-safe strategy for revolution, but it has got enough content to exclude certain apparent possibilities, and so takes us further than a mere empiricist politics of wait-and-see. For example, Marxist theory (as developed by Lenin) excludes the 'possibility' of a parliamentary road to socialism (PRS). The question about the epistemological status of Marxism can be made more concrete by looking at this example.

In the first place, one must avoid the temptation of looking for direct empirical verification of this doctrine – for example in Chile. Someone can always give plausible reasons for thinking that Chile was a special case. And Lenin had already long since formulated the essentials of the case against the possibility of a PRS. But on the other hand this is not something that follows in rationalistic fashion from *a priori* definitions. This could hardly be so when, as is well known, Marx and Engels, in historical conditions rather different from today's, *did* believe a PRS to be possible in a few countries (Britain, USA, Holland – see Engels' introduction to *Class Struggles in France*, and Marx's speech on the Hague Congress of the First International – both postdating the Paris Commune).

The impossibility of the PRS follows from the nature of the state apparatus in advanced bourgeois societies. Not primarily the nature of parliament itself, but of army, bureaucracy, police etc. When Marx and Engels envisaged a PRS, they nevertheless recognized that all that an electoral victory for a revolutionary workers' party would do is show that class consciousness had reached the point of ripeness for workers' power, it would not in itself constitute that power. A 'pro-slavery rebellion' on the part of the bourgeoisie could be expected. By the time of the Russian revolution it was obvious to Lenin that the parliamentary democracies had developed sufficiently large, specialized, powerful and hierarchical state apparatuses to remove the struggle for power from the parliamentary site altogether (which does not mean that the workers' movement cannot use parliament, as the bourgeoisie does, for *ideological* purposes). The confrontation between classes in future revolutionary situations therefore would take the form, not primarily of confrontations between parties in parliament, but between the whole hierarchy of bourgeois state and economic apparatuses on the one hand, and a network of democratic workers' institutions – workers' councils, militias etc. – on the other. The essential difference between a parliament and the supreme representative assembly in a workers' state would be, not merely the class composition or mode of election (though those are of course important), but that the workers' assembly would rest on a pyramid of *democratic* organs of power (economic, military and administrative), whereas the bourgeois parliament rests on a *hierarchic* apparatus. The crucial divide between Lenin and the believer in the PRS then consists in their view of the nature of the organs of state power in bourgeois democracies. Are they simply instruments which can be transferred from bourgeois to proletarian hands, or are they essentially institutions of bourgeois power which must be smashed? Once the question has been put in this form (a Marxist form, determined by the higher-level – but still empirical – hypothesis that all states are forms of class power) it can be answered by investigating the daily running of bourgeois states. All sorts of empirical facts – about Watergate, the refusal of army chiefs in Ulster to obey their parliamentary masters, the approval given by the organs of the British bourgeoisie (*The Times*, *The Economist*) to the Chilean atrocities, the co-operation of police chiefs with the fascists at Lewisham and Manchester, a judge giving his blessing to an advocate of genocide – these facts acquire a theoretical importance far beyond that granted them by the liberal who sees in them only 'abuses'.

The structure of the epistemology governing our revolutionary theory then is as follows: our theoretical postulates are tested, not indeed under laboratory conditions, but not merely by applying them in revolutionary practice either. They generate questions which can be asked of the various realities thrown up by history, such that the answers that history gives[22] are not just facts, but evidence for the theoretical postulates, which can then be used to guide strategy in new circumstances too. May one never have to prove the poisonous pudding of the PRS in the manner of the Chilean comrades – by eating it.

Notes

1 I admit to feeling that it is somewhat shameful to be reiterating this position at a time when one needs to break new ground in scientific epistemology, and when philosophers such as Roy Bhaskar are doing so (see his *A Realist Theory of Science*). But it is a shameful necessity, for while idealism enjoys a revival unparalleled since Edwardian times – and precisely among self-styled radicals – really new knowledge will be prevented from having the political effects that it deserves.

What is most disconcerting is that modern idealists are not only unaware that their sophisms have long since been refuted; they are even unaware that they are idealists. Who can doubt that if Bishop Berkeley had been alive today he would have re-titled his major work 'Towards a Materialist Theory of Perception'?

2 'Historicist' not in any Popperian sense, but in that it reduces a theory *about* a social practice to an epiphenomenon of that social practice, thus replacing epistemological questions about the truth of the theory by questions about its historical actuality, origin, function etc.

3 As I am criticizing 'spontaneism' in epistemology, I should perhaps say that I do not think Luxemburg was guilty of it, despite both the allegations of Althusser and the claims of some of her would-be followers. Her criticism of German Social Democracy expresses the same conception of the relation of theory to practice as Lenin's, and nothing in her critique of Lenin's views on party organization implies the opposite. Indeed she convicts Lenin himself of one spontaneist error: his positive evaluation of the effects of factory discipline on proletarian ideology.

4 The note in question contains a number of (undialectical) contradictions, but on one point it is clear: that Althusser has conceded the entire case to the historicists. The materialist interpretation of epistemology, he tells us 'could lead us to study the material, social, political, ideological and philosophical conditions of the theoretical "modes of production" and "production processes" of already existing knowledge: but this would properly fall within the domain of Historical Materialism!'

5 Althusser does place science outside the superstructure. But it is not necessary to do so in order to avoid historicism, as I hope my next paragraph shows. The 'scientific community', its institutions and practices, its relations with various state and economic apparatuses etc. are quite obviously part of the social formation in question, and as such part of the object of historical materialism. I am sure that Althusser did not intend his denial of science's place in the super-structure to deny this, but it can only give that impression. When he

99

finally asserts it – as quoted in my last note – it is to sell the pass to historicism.

It is extraordinary how strong is the prejudice that if one practice can be known by virtue of another, the former loses its autonomy and is explained away by the other. I can only assume that there is some primary-process thinking here – perhaps an infantile identification of knowledge with eating.

6   A scientist will often be tempted to explain a concrete reality wholly in terms of concepts belonging to his own theory, when in fact laws belonging to other scientific areas are (also) effective in generating that reality. He may then unnecessarily revise his own theory to accommodate the facts in question. Thus, the First World War is for the most part explicable in terms of historical materialism, yet Freud may well have postulated the death-wish in order to allow it to be accounted for in psychoanalytic terms.

When such an error is made, it is legitimate for the science possessing the real explanation to criticize the other science, including its new abstract postulates (the death-wish) in order to retrieve the stray effect of its own object.

But when a science tries to extend itself into an area from which it has necessarily abstracted in constituting its own object – as when 'Marxist theories of psychology' are propounded – one gets nothing but theoretically childish and practically pernicious rubbish.

7   Though traces of earlier (rationalist, empiricist or idealist) epistemologies persist in all these scientific epistemologies. In Althusser's case, he fails to completely free himself from rationalist elements. Later in this essay I shall touch on the epistemological effects of these rationalist residues, but it is worth noting that they have other effects as well. For instance, he makes fun of Plekhanov 'who ransacked Louis XV's bed to prove that the secrets of the fall of the *Ancien Régime* were not hidden there. As a general rule, concepts are not hidden in beds'. (*Reading Capital*, p. 112). Quite, and they do not start revolutions, either.

8   With important provisos about its interpretation. In *Lenin and Philosophy* this definition appears in an interpretation compatible with materialist epistemology; in *Essays in Self-Criticism* it leads to its abandonment.

9   According to Annenkov, Weitling was explaining that 'his aim was not to create new economic theories but to adopt those that were most appropriate, as experience in France had shown, to open the eyes of the workers to the horrors of their condition'. Marx objected that 'to rouse the population without giving them any firm, well-thought-out reasons for their activity would be simply to deceive them'. Weitling consoled himself 'by the thought that his modest spadework was perhaps of greater weight for the common cause than criticism and armchair analysis of doctrines far from the world of the suffering and afflicted people'. At this, Marx left the table saying 'Ignorance never yet helped anybody!'. (Quoted in David McLellan's, *Karl Marx*, pp. 156–157).

10 A note on the terminology I shall be using is needed here.

I use the term 'essentialism' for the ontology implicit in rationalist epistemology. This is marked by (a) an intepretation of real relations in terms of logical relations between concepts (for example Spinoza's understanding of causality on the model of deductive relations between propositions), and (b) the conception of a complex process as the expression of an essence, for example Leibniz's doctrine that all the vicissitudes of a monad are necessarily entailed by its eternal essence, just as all the parts of a curve are generated by the equation it expresses. This Leibnizian notion, the 'expressive totality', re-appears in Kant's argument for the completeness of the table of categories, and in Hegel's conception of a civilization as an embodiment of a single idea.

By 'holism' I refer to the application of this last Leibnizian doctrine to society; according to holism in this sense, the elements of a society are wholly constituted by that society, and are explicable without residue in social terms. This doctrine, for which individuals are 'unreal', mere 'aspects' of society, has been used politically – for example by Italian fascism.

By 'teleology' I mean explanations of a process by its result, explanations of what happens in terms of an 'in order to . . . '. For instance: 'species developed lungs in order to breath air' or 'the medieval church preached punishment in the hereafter in order to keep the peasants in subjection'. An example of teleology in recent Marxist thought is the idea that there is no socialist mode of production, it is merely the transition between capitalism and communism, as if the end (communism) could determine the nature of the intermediate society. The denial of teleology does not of course commit us to denying that people have purposes. It means that purposes are something to be explained, and teleological expressions will disappear in the explanation.

11 There are, of course, homoeostatic mechanisms in nature. I wonder if these authors would regard them as teleological, or pretend they do not exist.

12 This intentionally vague term is intended to include at least the mature Marx, Engels, Lenin, Luxemburg and Trotsky, and to exclude historicist Marxism, whether of the Stalinist variety (Soviet Marxism in the 1930s and 1940s was profoundly historicist), or the Western Hegelian variety (Korsch, Lukacs, Gramsci, the Frankfurt school, Sartre).

13 It may seem odd that I treat mechanistic atomism as a *bona fide* form of materialism when applied to the natural world, but as failing to provide a materialist account of society (even an inadequate one). Was Hobbes' account of society not a materialist one, even though false?

My reason is that the choice of human individuals as the irreducible atoms of society is unjustifiable on materialist grounds. In the idea that the motives and powers of human individuals can be explained purely internally, without reference to the effects of their socially

specific relations of dependence, there is a powerful residue of
idealist conceptions of the soul and free will.

14   It might be thought by 'humanistic' Marxists that there is an alternative to Hegelian and atomistic social explanations other than the
one that I defend here–namely, that the explanatory structures of
capitalist society are 'reified praxis'. In that case I would want to know:
How does this praxis get reified? Is it self-reifying? In that case one is
back with Hegel, and the objectivity, 'coefficient of adversity' and
sheer cussedness of capitalist reality are not given their due. Is it the
activity of the capitalists that reifies the praxis of the workers? In
that case, one would be back with an atomistic account of some
individuals oppressing others; unless this is a way of saying that the
structure of capitalist society (which constitutes the capitalists as
capitalists) has this effect. But in that case one is back with the notion
of an objective structure, independent of the will and consciousness of
individuals, which is the concept I am defending.

On the misuse of the word 'reification', see note 20 below.

15   These authors are aware that their views will be seen as idealist,
and as I said at the beginning, are keen to deny this interpretation.
It is worth looking at a few passages in *Mode of Production and Social
Formation* in which Hindess and Hirst try to distinguish their position
from idealism:

(a) We must insist, confident that we shall be misread, that our
rejection of the epistemological category of 'concrete' is not a
denial of the significance or reality of (material) objects. That
denial is a position within epistemology which substitutes other
(spiritual) objects as appropriate to knowledge. We do not deny
the *existence* of social relations–that would render our project
absurd. What we reject is the *category* of 'concrete' as object-of-
knowledge. It is the relation of 'appropriation' or of 'correspondence' of knowledge to its objects which we challenge.
(pp. 6–7).

Three things can be said about this:

(i) Idealism is taken here in the sense of idealist *ontology*, where it is
idealist *epistemology* which is at issue. The two are logically independent.

(ii) Saying that their position is not idealist because it is not
epistemology is as fatuous as A. J. Ayer's claim that he is not an
atheist since in his view it makes no sense to talk of God, and would
therefore make no sense to deny his existence.

(iii) The non-existence of social relations would render their
project no more absurd than would the non-correspondence of
knowledge and its objects.

(b) This does not commit us to denying that tables exist (so said
Berkeley–A.C.) or cause us intellectual discomfort when we

refrain from walking out of the top windows of high buildings. (p. 8).

I have lost no sleep worrying about the physical safety of Hindess and Hirst. If idealists acted on their sophisms, a Darwinian process would have considerably simplified the task of materialist philosophers. Unfortunately the dislocation between theory and reality which idealism excuses does have practical effects at more complex levels. The elimination of the bigger part of Marxist theory in *Marx's Capital and Capitalism Today* could have very serious political effects if it convinced the left. In vol. II of the latter book, political conclusions are drawn (Cutler dissenting). They are not essentially different from Bennery.

(c) This is not to deny 'reality' exists, is ordered, or to assert that it is infinite and unknowable – all of these are sceptical or critical positions within epistemological discourse. (p. 8)

all epistemologies share the conception of an independently existing realm of objects that may nonetheless be correlated with their representations or appropriations in determinate forms of discourse. *To deny epistemology is to deny that correlation. It is not to deny forms of existence outside of discourse but it is to deny that existence takes the form of objects representable in discourse.* (p. 21).

If it is denied that reality is representable in discourse, it is asserted that reality is unknowable, despite protestations to the contrary. The gentlemen must make up their minds. If they think that knowledge has some relation to reality, they must tell us what it is. If not, they must say what the point of knowledge is. If they cannot, they should shut up.

16 I sometimes get the impression, from the manner and frequency with which they repeat this formula for epistemology as *both* distinctness *and* correspondence of the two realms, that they think that distinctness in itself precludes correspondence, and that the epistemological project therefore only has to be expressed this way in order to be refuted. This would be on a level with the idea that one cannot have any knowledge of other people's mental states, as one cannot introspect them.

17 To avoid a possible misinterpretation: I have no sympathy for historicist readings of Kant, which have found some favour among Marxists (for example Lucien Goldman). According to such views, one does indeed shape reality in the process of knowing it, but in socially determined and historically relative ways. The 'inversion' which I favour is the opposite of this: a realist insistence on the objectivity of knowledge, a denial that reality is our product; and consequently a re-interpretation of the status of the so-called 'synthetic *a priori*',

which remains as the set of the conditions of the possibility of experience (knowledge), but contingently and objectively realized conditions.

18   The question 'How are non-teleological self-reproducing structures possible?' is best answered by referring to actual structures of this kind – to answer it in general terms is to risk falling into the sort of *a priori* dialectics which was the chief error of the older forms of dialectical materialism (from Engels to Mao). If the detailed account of the reproduction of capitalist social relations in Marx's *Capital* does not convince these authors, I can only suppose an *a priori* rejection of dialectics on their part, and recommend that they take another look at modern biology.

.However there do exist some general accounts of this kind of structure, produced independently of Althusser's account. For instance in Bukharin's much maligned *Historical Materialism*, and, in exposition of Spinoza, in Hans Jonas's paper 'Spinoza and the Theory of Organism', in *Spinoza: a Collection of Critical Essays*, Marjorie Grene (ed.).

19   'Specialized' in the sense that it is distinct from other activities, not necessarily in the sense of being the activity of a socially distinct body of specialists. Naturally, in a bourgeois society, the social division of labour is superimposed on the technical division, and the 'scientific community' as a rule forms part of the bourgeoisie or petty bourgeoisie. This does not of course mean that the contents of their discoveries are bourgeois, any more than one can taste the surplus value in ones beer.

Having said that though, I certainly do not imagine that communist society could do without 'experts'. The simple fact that human knowledge accumulates necessitates the permanent increase of specialization. The anti-specialism lobby stems from a petty bourgeois conception of knowledge as the private property of individuals.

20   It has been suggested to me that referring to the objects of science as 'things' is revealing, indicating some 'reification' underlying my thought. The expression I use was suggested by the phrases '*res ipsa loquitur*' and 'to the things themselves' (the latter a translation of Husserl's 'Zu den Sachen').

But as this is a common objection to the 'scientistic' Marxism which it is my concern to defend, it is worthy of a few comments. The OED gives as the primary sense of 'thing': 'whatever is or may be an object of thought', and derives it from Old High German 'ding' meaning 'public assembly'. Equivalent words in other European languages also indicate a primary sense of 'object of discourse or activity' rather than 'bit of hardware', which is what people have in mind in connection with 'reification'.

In common usage, 'thing' is the most general ontological term in the English language, ranging over events ('a funny thing happened to me . . . '), people ('you poor old thing'), statements, actions ('what a thing to say, do'), relationships ('baby, we've got a good thing going'), intellectual problems ('The time has come the walrus said, to speak of many things ... why the sea is boiling hot and whether pigs have wings')–the list could be extended indefinitely.

Two 'things' (conclusions) follow from this. (1) The term 'reification' will be quite contentless unless one restricts its meaning to something like 'the fallacy of misplaced concreteness'. (2) There is likely to be a hidden motive behind the objection to 'reifying' discourse (in the wider, contentless sense). I would suggest an epistemophobia which finds it threatening to be the object of knowledge (it is noteworthy that the word 'objectifying' is used of knowledge with the same pejorative sense). I would seriously suggest that the whole anti-scientific ideology which sees objective knowledge as a threat in this way can be explained without residue in Freudian terms as an effect of a reaction-formation against scopophilia. See Nietzsche: 'Science offends the modesty of all genuine women. They feel as if one were trying to look under their skin–or worse! under their clothes and finery.' (*Beyond Good and Evil*, p. 81). Needless to say, this does not only apply to women, let alone to 'genuine' women, whatever they might be.

21 This is because, in Bhaskarian terms, one is unable in the human sciences to actualize closure–even in the abstract parts of these sciences. The 'power of abstraction' of which Marx speaks, when unaided by methods of producing conditions of closure, cannot achieve accurate measurement.

22 In case there are any readers who still imagine that Marxists personify 'history' and spell it with a capital 'H', I should point out that it is a figure of speech similar to 'experience teaches us ... ' or 'time will tell'.

Bibliography

Althusser, Louis, *For Marx* (Harmondsworth 1969). *Lenin and Philosophy* (London 1971); *Politics and History* (London 1972); *Essays in Self-Criticism* (London 1976).

Althusser, Louis and Balibar, Etienne, *Reading Capital* (London 1970).

Bhaskar, Roy, *A Realist Theory of Science* (York 1975: 2nd ed., Hassocks 1978).

Bukharin, Nicolai, *Historical Materialism* (Ann Arbor 1969).

Callinicos, Alex, *Althusser's Marxism* (London 1976).

Cutler, Hindess, Hirst and Hussain, *Marx's Capital and Capitalism Today* I (London 1977), II (London 1978).

Engels, Friedrich, Preface to Marx's *Class Struggles in France* (Moscow 1972).

Geras, Norman, *The Legacy of Rosa Luxemburg* (London 1976).

Grene, Marjorie (ed.), *Spinoza : a Collection of Critical Essays* (New York 1973).

Hindess, Barry, *Philosophy and Methodology in the Social Sciences* (Hassocks 1977).

Hindess, Barry and Hirst, Paul, *Pre-Capitalist Modes of Production* (London 1975); *Mode of Production and Social Formation* (London 1977),

Husserl, Edmund, *Logical Investigations* (London 1970).

Kant, Immanuel, *Critique of Pure Reason* (London 1964).

Lenin, Vladimir, *What is to be Done?* (Moscow 1947); *Materialism and Empirio-Criticism* (Moscow 1947).

Mandel, Ernest, 'Revolutionary strategy in Europe', *New Left Review*, no. 100 (Nov. 1976–Jan. 1977).

Marx, Karl, *Grundrisse* (for 1857 Introduction) (Harmondsworth 1973); *Capital*, I (Harmondsworth 1976); *The First International and After* (for *The Civil War in France* and 'Speech on the Hague Congress') (Harmondsworth 1974).

Marx, Karl and Engels, Friedrich, *The German Ideology* (London 1970); *The Communist Manifesto* in *The Revolutions of 1848* (Harmondsworth 1973).

Nietzsce, Friedrich, *Beyond Good and Evil* (Harmondsworth 1973).

Popper, Karl, *The Open Society and its Enemies* (London 1945); *The Poverty of Historicism* (London 1957); *Objective Knowledge* (Oxford 1972).

Timpanaro, Sebastiano, *On Materialism* (London 1975).

Waters, Mary-Allice (ed.), *Rosa Luxemburg Speaks* (New York 1970).

On the Possibility of Social Scientific Knowledge and the Limits of Naturalism

ROY BHASKAR

Introduction

IN this paper I want to discuss an old question that refuses to lie down. It is a question that continually resurfaces in philosophical discussions on the social sciences and reappears, in one guise or another, in methodological discussions within them: *to what extent can society be studied in the same way as nature?* Without exaggerating, I think one could call this question the primal problem of the philosophy of the social sciences. For the history of that subject has been dominated by a dispute between two traditions. The first – a naturalistic tradition – has typically seen science as (actually or ideally) unified in its concordance with *positivist* principles, based in the last instance on the Humean notion of law. The second – a rival anti-naturalist tradition, of *hermeneutics* – has posited, by contrast, a radical distinction in method between the natural and social sciences, flowing from and grounded in the idea of a radical distinction in their subject matters. The philosophical lineage of this tradition is traceable back through Weber and Dilthey to the transcendental idealism of Kant. Within the Marxist camp an exactly parallel dispute has occurred, with the so-called 'dialectical materialists' on one side and Lukacs, the Frankfurt school and Sartre on the other.

Now, with the possible exception of the 'dialectical materialists' (whose specificity I do not want to discuss here), the great error that unites these disputants is their acceptance of an essentially positivist account of natural science, and more generally of an empiricist ontology. This is very evident if one looks at Peter Winch's *The idea of a Social Science*, perhaps the most influential tract written within the so-called 'analytical' school. Winch, it will be remembered, wants to argue that there is an essential identity between philosophy and social science, on the one hand, and a fundamental contrast between the latter and the natural sciences, on the other. When we turn to his arguments for such a contrast we find that they boil down to two. The first is an argument to the effect the constant conjunctions of events are neither sufficient nor (contrary to for example Weber) even necessary for social scientific explanation, which is achieved instead by the discovery of intelligible connections in its subject matter.[1] This may be granted. But the required contrast is only generated if one assumes that the discovery of intelligible connections in *its* subject matter is not equally the goal of natural scientific explanation. The second is an argument to the effect that social things have no existence, other than a purely physical existence, that is as social things, apart from the concepts that agents possess of them.[2] Besides leaving the ontological status of concepts unclear, once more the assumed contrast gets off the ground if one tacitly assumes that, with the privileged exception of thought itself, only material objects can properly be said to be 'real', that is that in natural science *esse est percipi*. Winch's anti-naturalism thus depends entirely on empiricist theories of existence and causality. By in effect ceding natural science to positivism, Winch precludes himself from locating the true differences between the natural and the social sciences. Lukacs in the Marxist tradition makes an exactly parallel mistake.

Now I think that recent developments in the philosophy of science allow,[3] as the current crisis in the social sciences necessitates, a reconsideration of the problem of naturalism. *Naturalism* may be defined as the thesis that there is (or can be) an essential unity of method between the natural and the social sciences. It must be straightaway distinguished from two species of it: *reductionism*, which posits an actual identity of subject matter as well; and *scientism*, which denies that there are any important differences in the methods appropriate to studying societies and nature, whether or not they are actually (as in reductionism) identified. In contrast to both these forms of naturalism I want to argue for a qualified anti-positivist naturalism. Such a naturalism holds that it is possible to give an account of science under which the proper and more or less specific methods of both the natural and social sciences can fall. But it does not deny that there are important differences in these methods, grounded in the real differences that exist in their subject matters. In particular it will be seen that *ontological*, *epistemological* and *relational* considerations reveal differences that place limits on the possibility of naturalism, or rather qualify the form it must take in the social sciences. Moreover these differences all carry methodological import. However, it will transpire that it is not in spite of, but rather just in *virtue of*, the real differences that distinguish the subject matter of the social from the natural sciences that social science is possible; that here, as elsewhere, it is the nature of the object that determines the form of its science. So that to investigate the limits of naturalism is *ipso facto* to investigate the conditions which make social science, whether or not it is actualized in practice, possible.

I want first to sketch the elements of an adequate account of natural science, in relation to which the possibility of social scientific knowledge can be re-appraised.

Transcendental realism and the problem of naturalism
I have argued elsewhere that it is a condition of the intelligibility of the experimental establishment and the practical application of knowledge that its objects are real structures which exist and act independently of the patterns of events they generate.[4] If follows from this that causal laws must be analysed as tendencies, which are only necessarily manifest in empirical invariances under realatively special closed conditions.[5] Thus, contrary to the specific claims of Popper and Hempel and the tacit presupposition of Winch, deducibility from empirical invariances, depending upon the availability of constant conjunctions of events, can be neither necessary nor sufficient for a natural scientific explanation. There is an ontological gap between causal laws and their empirical grounds, which both parties to the naturalist debate have hitherto ignored. This not only renders standard positivist methodological injunctions patently inapplicable, it also vitiates the most familiar hermeneutical contrasts. Thus just as a rule can be broken without being changed, so a

natural mechanism may continue to endure, and the law it grounds be both applicable and true (that is, not falsified), though its effect, that is the consequent, be unrealized.[6]

Knowledge, then, has 'intransitive' objects which exist and act independently of it. But it is itself a social process, whose aim is the production of the knowledge of such objects, that is of the mechanisms of the production of phenomena in nature. Now if we are to avoid the absurdity of the assumption of the production of such knowledge *ex nihilo* it must depend on the utilization of antecedently existing cognitive materials (which I have called the 'transitive' objects of knowledge). Typically, then, the construction of an explanation for some identified phenomenon will involve the building of a model, making use of such cognitive materials and operating under the control of something like a logic of analogy and metaphor,[7] of a mechanism, which *if* it were to exist and act in the postulated way would account for the phenomenon in question.[8] The reality of the posited explanation must then, of course, be subjected to empirical scrutiny (for in general more than one explanation will be consistent with the phenomenon concerned). Once done, it must then itself in principle be explained. And so there is in science a three-phase schema of development, in which in a continuing dialectic, science identifies a phenomenon (or range of phenomena), constructs explanations for it and empirically tests its explanations, leading to the identification of the generative mechanism at work, which now becomes the phenomenon to be explained, and so on. On this view of science its essence lies in the move at any one level from manifest phenomena to the structures that generate them. The question of naturalism can thus be posed as follows: to what extent is it possible to suppose that a comparable move can be made in the domain of the social sciences?

Now our analysis of science immediately pinpoints an internal difficulty in this project. For the objects of scientific inquiry are neither empirically given nor even actually determinate chunks of the world, but rather real structures, whose actual presence and appropriate concept have to be produced by the experimental and theoretical work of science. Thus it would seem that we must first know what kinds of things societies are before we can consider whether it is possible to

study them scientifically. Indeed without some prior specification of an object of inquiry, any discourse on method is
bound to be more or less arbitrary. The question to which this
paper aspires to make a contribution may therefore be set as
follows: what properties do societies possess that might make
them possible objects of knowledge for us?

In considering this question it is essential to establish that
these properties, and *a fortiori* their bearers, societies, are real.
For unless this is done our analysis of science entails that the
possibility of a non-reductionist naturalism must straightaway collapse. Now, in this respect, it is important to note that
science employs two criteria for the ascription of reality to a
posited object: a perceptual and a causal one. The latter turns
on the capacity of the entity whose existence is in doubt to
bring about changes in material things. It should be noticed
that a magnetic or gravitational field satisfies this criterion,
but not a criterion of perceivability. On this criterion to be is
not to be perceived, but (in the last instance) just to be able to
do.[9] The standard hermeneutical fork, turning on a concep-
tual/perceptible dichotomy, which we have already seen
invoked by Winch, ignores of course just the possibilities
opened up by a causal criterion for ascribing reality.

My strategy in this paper will be based on a pincer movement. First I will concentrate mainly on the ontological
question of the properties that societies possess. Then I will
shift to the epistemological question of how this might make
them objects of knowledge. In considering the former I want
to argue that society is irreducible to persons and to attempt a
sketch of their relationship. For my purpose merely to argue
against methodological individualism, though necessary, is
not sufficient. For one must show not only that in explanations
in the field of the human sciences social predicates are
irreducible, but that a realistic interpretation of social
scientific explanations is in principle acceptable; that is that
some possible objects designated by social scientific theory
are real.

Against methodological individualism
Methodological individualism asserts that facts about society
and social phenomena are to be explained solely in terms of

facts about individuals. For Popper, for example, 'all social
phenomena, and especially the functioning of social institutions, should be understood as resulting from the decisions
etc. of human individuals . . . we should never be satisfied by
explanations in terms of so-called "collectives".'[10] Social
institutions are merely 'abstract models' designed to interpret
the facts of individual experience. As Jarvie has put it:
'"army" is just the plural of "soldier" and all statements about
the army can be reduced to statements about the particular
soldiers comprising it'.[11] Watkins concedes that 'there may be
unfinished or half-way explanations of large-scale phenomena
in terms of other large-scale phenomena (such as of inflation
in terms of full employment)',[12] but contends that one will
not have arrived at so-called 'rock-bottom' (ultimate?)
explanations of such phenomena until they are deduced from
statements about the dispositions, beliefs, resources and
interrelations of individuals.[13] Specifically, social events are
to be explained by deducing them from the principles governing the behaviour of the 'participating' individuals,[14] together
with statements of their situations. In this way, methodological individualism stipulates the *material* conditions for
adequate explanation in the social sciences to complement
the *formal* ones laid down by the deductive – nomological
model.

Now when one considers the range of predicates applicable
to individuals and individual behaviour – from those that
designate properties, such as shape and texture, that people
possess in common with other material objects, through those
that pick out states, such as hunger and pain, that they share
with other higher animals, to those that designate actions that
are, as far as one knows, uniquely characteristic of them – the
real problem appears to be not so much of how one could give
an individualistic explanation of social behaviour, but that of
how one could give a non-social (that is strictly individualistic) explanation of individual, at least characteristically
human, behaviour![15] For the predicates designating properties special to persons all presuppose a social context for
their employment. A tribesman implies a tribe, the cashing
of a cheque a banking system. Explanation, whether by
subsumption under general laws, advertion to motives and

rules, or by redescription (identification), always seems to involve irreducibly social predicates.

Moreover it is not difficult to show that the arguments adduced in support of methodological individualism will not bear the weight placed upon them. For example, a comparison of the motives of a criminal with the procedures of a court is sufficient to show that facts about individuals are neither necessarily more observable nor necessarily easier to understand than social phenomena. Again, a comparison of the concepts of love and war shows that concepts applicable to individuals are not necessarily either clearer or easier to define than those that designate social phenomena.

Significantly, the qualifications and refinements proposed by the advocates of methodological individualism weaken rather than strengthen the case for it. Thus the admission of ideal types etc. weakens the force of the ontological considerations in favour of it, while allowing 'half-way' and statistical explanations undermines the epistemological ones. Moreover the examples cited of supposedly genuinely 'holistic' behaviour, such as riots and the biological union of mating couples,[16] merely reveal the poverty of their implicit conception of the social. For, upon analysis of their writing, it is clear that most methodological individualists regard 'the social' as a synonym for 'the group'. The issue for them, then, becomes that of whether society, the whole, is greater than the sum of its constituent parts, individual men. Social behaviour, on this view, then becomes explicable as the behaviour of groups of individuals or of individuals in groups.

Now I think that this definition of the social is radically misconceived: sociology is not concerned, as such, with large-scale, mass or group behaviour, conceived as the behaviour of large numbers, masses or groups of individuals, but (paradigmatically) with the persistent *relations* between individuals (and groups), and with the relations between these relations. Relations such as between capitalist and worker, MP and constituent, student and teacher, husband and wife. Now such relations are general and relatively enduring but they do not involve collective or mass behaviour as such in the way in which a strike or a demonstration does (though of course they may help to explain the latter). Mass behaviour is an interesting social psychological phenomenon, but it is not the subject matter of sociology.

Now what makes this situation particularly ironical is that the more sophisticated methodological individualists formally concede that relations must play some role in explanation. What then accounts for the polemics and the passion? I think that it can only be explained in terms of their desire to defend a particular form of substantive social scientific explanation, which they mistakenly hold to be uniquely consistent with political liberalism. As Watkins himself has put it: 'Since Mandeville's *Fable of the Bees* was published in 1714, individualistic social science, with its emphasis on unintended consequences has largely been a sophisticated elaboration on the simple theme that, in certain situations, selfish private motives [that is capitalism] may have good social consequences and good political intentions [that is socialism] bad social consequences'.[17] There is in fact one body of social doctrine, whose avatars are utilitarianism, liberal political theory, pre-Ricardian classical and neo-classical economic theory, that does conform to individualistic prescriptions, on the assumption that what is in effect a generalized aggregation problem can be solved. According to this model reason is the efficient slave of the passions[18] and social behaviour can be seen as the outcome of a simple maximization problem or its dual, a minimization one: the application of reason, the sole identifying characteristic of man, to desires (appetites and aversions, in Hobbes) or feelings (pleasure and pain, in Hume, Bentham and Mill) that may be regarded as neurophysiologically given. Relations play no part in this model; and this model, if it applies at all, applies as much to Crusoe as to socialized man, and to man whatever (that is wherever and whenever) his socialisation – with the corollary expressed by Hume that 'mankind is much the same at all times and places'.[19]

The limitations of this approach to social science should by now be well known. To say that men are rational does not explain *what* they do, but only at best (that is supposing that an objective function could be reconstructed for their behaviour and empirically tested independently of it) *how* they do it. Rationality, purporting to explain everything, ends up explaining nothing. To explain a human action by reference to its rationality is like explaining some natural event by reference to its being caused. Rationality is, in this sense, a presupposition of investigation. As for neo-classical economic theory, the most developed form of this tendency in social thought, it may best be regarded as a normative theory of efficient action, generating a set of techniques for achieving given ends, rather than as an explanatory theory capable of casting light on actual empirical episodes. That is, as a praxiology,[20] not a sociology.

Aside from its championship of a particular explanation form, methodological individualism derives plausibility from the fact that it seems to touch on an important truth, awareness of which accounts for its apparent necessity: namely the idea that society is made up of or consists of and only of people. In what sense is this true? In the sense that the material presence of social effects consists only in changes in people and changes brought about by people on other material things – objects of nature, such as land, and artefacts produced by work on objects of nature. One could express this truth as follows: *the material presence of society = persons and the (material) results of their actions*. It is this truth that the methodological individualists have glimpsed, only to shroud it with their apologetic shifts.

It is clear that there is, in methodological individualism, a sociological reductionism and a psycho-(or praxio)logical atomism at work, exactly paralleling with respect to the content of explanation, the theoretical reductionism and ontological atomism determining its form. In the philosophy of social science the sociology of individualism plays as important a role in defining the object of investigation as the ontology of empiricism does in defining its method. Together I think that they must be held largely responsible (or rather, they theoretically reflect whatever is responsible) for the social scientific malaise.

The *relational* conception of the subject matter of sociology advocated here may be contrasted not only with the *individualist* conception, exemplified, for example by utilitarian social theory, but with what I shall call the *collectivist* conception, best exemplified perhaps by the work of Durkheim, with its heavy emphasis on the concept of the group. Durkheim's group is not of course the same as Popper's. It is, to use a Sartrean analogy, more of the nature of a fused group than a series.[21] In particular, as definitive of the social, it is characterized by the possession of certain emergent powers, whose justification I will consider below. Nevertheless the key concepts of the Durkheimian corpus, such as conscience collective, organic *vs.* mechanical solidarity, anomie etc. all derive their meaning from their relationship to the concept of the collective nature of social phenomena. Thus, for Durkheim, to the extent at least that he is to remain committed to positivism, enduring relationships must be reconstructed from collective phenomena; whereas on the realist and relational view advanced here collective phenomena are seen primarily as the expressions of enduring relationships. Note that on this conception sociology is not only not essentially concerned with the group, it is not even essentially concerned with behaviour.

If Durkheim combined a collectivist conception of sociology with a positivist methodology, Weber combined a neo-Kantian methodology with a still essentially individualist conception of sociology. His break from utilitarianism is primarily at the level of the forms of action or types of behaviour he is prepared to recognize, not at the level of the unit of study. It is significant that just as the thrust contained in Durkheim's isolation of the emergent properties of the group is constrained by his continuing commitment to an empiricist methodology, so the possibilities opened up by Weber's isolation of the ideal type are constrained by his continuing commitment to an empiricist ontology.[22] In both cases a residual empiricism holds back, and ultimately annuls, a real scientific advance. For it is as futile to attempt to sustain a concept of the social on the basis of the category of the group, as it is to attempt to sustain a concept of natural necessity on the basis of the category of experience. Marx, I think, did make the attempt to combine a realist ontology and a relational sociology.[23] One can thus schematize four tendencies in social thought as in Table 1 below.

TABLE 1

	Method	Object
Utilitarianism	empiricist	individualist
Weber	neo-Kantian	individualist
Durkheim	empiricist	collectivist
Marx	realist	relational

n.b. concepts of method (social epistemology) under-pinned by general ontology; concepts of object (social ontology) underpinned by general epistemology.

It should be noted that as the relations between the relations that constitute the proper subject matter of sociology may themselves be *internally related* only the category of *totality* can express this. Some problems that this gives rise to will be considered below. But now I want to consider the nature of the connection between society and people.

Four models of the society/person relationship
It is customary to draw a divide between two camps in socio-logical theory: one, represented above all by Weber, in which social objects are seen as the results of (or as constituted by) intentional or meaningful human behaviour; and the other, represented by Durkheim, in which they are seen as possess-ing a life of their own, external to and coercing the individual. With some stretching the various schools of social thought – phenomenology, existentialism, structuralism, etc. – can then be seen as instances of one or other of these positions. And various brands of Marxism can then also be neatly classified. These two stereotypes can be represented as in the diagrams below.

Model I : The Weberian stereotype 'Voluntarism'

Model II : The Durkheimian stereotype 'Reification'

Now it is tempting to try to develop a general model capable of synthesizing these conflicting perspectives, on the assumption of a dialectical inter-relationship between society and men. I want to discuss a plausible variant of such a model, advocated most convincingly by Peter Berger and his associates.[24] Its weaknesses will, I think, enable us to work our way to a more adequate conception of the relationship between society and men, as well as to better display the errors of the conventional stereotypes.

According to the Berger model, which I shall call Model III, society forms the individuals who create society; society, that is, produces men, who produce society, in a continuous dialectic. Model III can be represented by the following diagram.

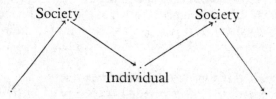

Society   Society

Individual

Model III : The 'Dialectical' conception

According to the proponents of this model 'social structure is not characterisable as a thing able to stand on its own, apart from the human activity that produced it'.[25] But equally, once created, 'it is encountered by the individual [both] as an alien facticity [and] . . . as a coercive instrumentality'.[26] 'It is *there*, impervious to his wishes, . . . other than [and resistant to] himself.'[27] This schema thus seems able to do justice both to the subjective and intentional aspects of social life and to the externality and coercive power of social facts. In this way any voluntaristic implications of the Weberian tradition and any reification associated with the Durkheimian one are simultaneously avoided; for a radical distinction is now drawn between natural and social facts, in that the latter but not the former do not exist independently of human activity.

Thus while agreeing with Durkheim that 'the system of signs I use to express my thoughts, the system of currency I employ to pay my debts, the instruments of credit I utilize in my commercial relations, the practices followed in my profession etc. function independently of my use of them,'[28] advocates of this model regard such systems, instruments and practices as *objectivations* that, under certain conditions, take on an alienated form. According to them objectivation is 'the process whereby human subjectivity embodies itself in products that are available to oneself and one's fellow men as elements of a common world'[29] and 'alienation is the process whereby the unity of the producing and the product is broken.'[30] Thus languages, forms of economic and political organization, cultural and ethical norms are all ultimately embodiments of human subjectivity. And any consciousness which does not see them as such is necessarily reified. Reification must, however, be distinguished from *objectivication*. This is necessary to any conceivable social life and is defined as 'the moment in the process of objectivation in which man establishes distance from his producing and its product, such that he can take cognizance of it and make of it an object of his consciousness'.[31]

On Model III, then, society is an objectivation or externalization of man. And man, for his part, is an internalization or re-appropriation in consciousness of society. Now I think that this model is seriously misleading. For it encourages, on the one hand, a voluntaristic idealism with respect to our understanding of social structure and, on the other, a mechanistic determinism with respect to our understanding of people. People and society are not, I shall argue, related 'dialectically'. They do not constitute two moments of the same process. Rather they refer to radically different kinds of thing.

Let us consider society. To return for a moment to Durkheim. It will be remembered that, reminding us that the church-member, or let us say the language-user, finds the beliefs and practices of his religious life, or the structure of his language, ready-made at birth, he argues that it is their existence *prior* to his own that implies their existence *outside* himself, and from which their coercive power is ultimately derived.[32] Now if this is the case and the social structure, and the natural world in so far as it is appropriated by men, is always *already made*, then Model III must be corrected in a fundamental way. It is still true to say that society would not exist without human activity, so that reification remains an error. And it is still true to say that such activity would not occur unless the agents engaging in it had a conception of what they were doing.[33] But it is no longer true to say that men *create* it. Rather we must say: They *reproduce* or *transform* it. That is to say, if society is already made, then any concrete human praxis or, if you like, act of objectivation can only modify it; and the totality of such acts sustain or change it. It is not the product of their activity (any more than their actions are completely determined by it). Society stands to individuals, then, as something that they never make, but that exists only in virtue of their activity.

The alternative model I propose, Model IV, may thus be expressed as follows: Men do not create society. For it always pre-exists them. Rather it is an ensemble of structures, practices and conventions that individuals reproduce or transform, but which would not exist unless they did so. Society does not exist independently of conscious human activity (the error of reification). But it is not the product of the latter (the error of voluntarism). This model may be represented diagrammatically as below.

Society

reproduction/ transformation

Individuals

Model IV : The transformational model of social activity

What is the counterpart, represented by the downward vertical lines, to the relationship of reproduction/transformation in which individuals stand to society? Society provides the necessary conditions for intentional human activity (as well as, in any given case, to a greater or lesser extent circumscribing its form). The processes whereby the stock of skills and competences appropriate to given social contexts are acquired could be generically referred to as 'socialization'. Notice that on Model I there are actions, but no conditions; on Model II conditions but no actions; on Model III no distinction between the two. Thus in Durkheim subjectivity tends to appear only in the guise of the interiorized form of social constraint. But a moment's reflection shows equally that real subjectivity requires conditions under which, and materials (for example language) with which, the subject can act.

It should be noted that Model IV, as a result of its emphasis on material continuity, can sustain a genuine concept of *change*, and hence of *history*[34] – something that neither Model I nor the methodological stereotypes it attempts to situate as special cases can do. Thus Model I appears to involve continuous recreation with genuine novelty, seemingly entailing incomplete social formation, something of a mystery. On the Weberian methodological stereotype change reduces to contrast, and on the Durkheimian one it can only be explained by adversion to exogenous variables. Model IV, moreover generates a clear criterion of historically significant events: viz. those that initiate or constitute ruptures, mutations or more generally transformations in social forms (such as Dalton's training as a meteorologist or the French Revolution).

Some emergent properties of social systems
Now if society pre-exists the individual, objectivation takes on a very different significance. For it, conscious human activity consists in work on *given* objects, and cannot be conceived as taking place in their absence. These objects may be material or ideational. And they may be regarded as the results of prior objectivations. Now this suggests a radically different conception of social activity, an essentially Aristotelian one: the paradigm being that of a sculptor at work, fashioning a product out of the material and with the tools available to him. I shall call this the transformational model of social activity. It applies to discursive as well as to non-discursive practices; to science and politics, as much as to economics. Thus in science the raw materials used in the construction of new theories are established results, half-forgotten ideas, the stock of available paradigms and models, methods and techniques of inquiry; so that the scientific innovator comes to appear in retrospect as a kind of cognitive *bricoleur*.[35] To use the Aristotelian terms, then, in every process of productive

activity a material as well as an efficient cause is necessary. And social activity consists, then, at least paradigmatically in work on and the transformation of given materials.

If such work constitutes the analogue of natural events, then one needs an analogue for the mechanisms that generate them. If social structures constitute the appropriate mechanism-analogue then one must at once register an important difference – in that, unlike natural mechanisms, they exist only in virtue of the activities they govern and cannot be empirically identified independently of them. Because of this they must be social products themselves. Thus men in their social activity must perform a double function: they must not only make social products but make the conditions of their making, that is reproduce (or to a greater or lesser extent transform) the structures governing their substantive activities of production. Because social structures are themselves social products, they are themselves possible objects of transformation and so may be only relatively enduring. And because social activities are interdependent, social structures may be only relatively autonomous. Society may thus be conceived as an articulated ensemble of such relatively independent and enduring structures; that is, as a complex totality subject to change both in its components and their interrelations. Moreover it is important to note that because social structures exist only in virtue of the activities they govern, they do not exist independently of the conceptions that the agents possess of what they are doing in their activity; that is of some theory of these activities. Finally, because social structures are themselves social products, social activity must be given a social explanation, and cannot be explained by reference to non-social parameters (though the latter may impose constraints on the possible forms of social activity).

Some ontological limitations on a possible naturalism in the domain of the social sciences can be immediately derived from these emergent social properties, on the assumption (to be vindicated in the next section) that society is *sui generis* real:

(1) social structures, unlike natural structures, do not exist independently of the activities they govern;

(2) social structures, unlike natural structures, do not exist

independently of the agents' conceptions of what they
are doing in their activity;

(3) social structures, unlike natural structures, may be only
relatively enduring (so that the tendencies they ground
may not be universal in the sense of space-time
invariant).[36]

These all indicate real differences in the possible objects of
knowledge in the case of the natural and social sciences. They
are not of course unconnected. Though one should be wary of
drawing conclusions of the sort: 'Society exists only in virtue
of human activity. Human activity is conscious. Therefore
consciousness brings about change.' For (a) social changes
need not be consciously intended and (b) if there are social
conditions for consciousness, change in it can in principle be
socially explained. Society, then, is an articulated ensemble
of tendencies and powers which, unlike natural ones, exist
only as long as they (or at least some of them) are being
exercised; are exercised in the last instance via the intentional
activity of men; and are not necessarily space-time invariant.

To turn now to people. Human action is characterized by
the striking phenomenon of intentionality. This seems to stem
from the fact that persons are material things with a degree of
neuro-physiological complexity which enables them not just,
like the higher animals, to initiate changes in a purposeful
way, to monitor and control their performances, but to
monitor the monitoring of these performances and to be
capable of a commentary upon them.[37] This capacity for
second-order monitoring also makes possible a retrospective
commentary upon actions, which gives a person's own
account of his behaviour a special status, which is acknow-
ledged in the best practice of all the psychological sciences.

The importance of distinguishing, in the most categorical
way, between human action and the social structure will now
be apparent. For the properties possessed by social forms may
be very different from those possessed by the individuals
upon whose activity they depend. For instance one can
suppose without paradox or tension that purposefulness,
intentionality and sometimes self-consciousness characterize
human action, but not changes in the social structure. I want
to distinguish sharply then between the genesis of human

actions, lying in the reasons, intentions and plans of men, on the one hand; and the structures governing the reproduction and transformation of social activities on the other; and hence between the domains of the psychological and the social sciences. The problem of how men reproduce any particular society belongs to a linking science of social psychology. It should be noted that engagement in social activity is itself a conscious human action which may, in general, be described either in terms of the agent's reasons for engaging in it or in terms of its social function or role.

Now the autonomy of the social and the psychological does justice to our intuitions. Thus one does not suppose that the reason why garbage is collected is necessarily the garbage collectors reason for collecting it (though it depends upon the latter). And one can allow that speech is governed by the rules of grammar without supposing either that these rules exist independently of speech habits (reification) or that they determine what one says. The rules of grammar, like natural structures, impose *limits* upon the speech acts that we can perform, but they do not *determine* our performances. One great advantage of this conception of social science is thus that it preserves the status of human agency, while doing away with the myth of creation (logical or historical), which depends upon the possibility of an individualist reduction. And in so doing it allows us to see that necessity in social life operates in the last instance via the intentional activity of man. Looked at in this way, then, one may regard it as the task of the various social sciences to lay out the structural conditions for various forms of conscious action – for example, what economic processes must take place for Christmas shopping to be possible – but they do not describe the latter.

To return once again to the relationship between society and people. The conception I am proposing is that people, in their conscious human activity, for the most part unconsciously reproduce (or occasionally, transform) the structures that govern their substantive activities of production. Thus people do not marry to reproduce the nuclear family, or work to reproduce the capitalist economy. But it is nevertheless the unintended consequence (and inexorable result) of, as it is also the necessary condition for, their activity.

On the reality of society and the subject matter of sociology

I now want to return to the question of the ontological status of societies. I have argued elsewhere that living things determine the conditions of applicability of the physical laws to which they are subject, so that their properties cannot be reduced to the latter; that is, that emergence characterizes both the natural and the human worlds.[38] (And that this is consistent with what may be termed a 'diachronic explanatory reduction', that is a reconstruction of the historical processes of their formation out of 'simpler' things.) If intentional action is a necessary condition for certain determinate states of the physical world, then the properties and powers that persons possess in virtue of which intentionality is correctly attributed to them are real. Similarly, if it can be shown that but for society, certain physical actions would not be performed, then, employing the causal criterion set out at the beginning, one is justified in asserting that it is real.

Now I think that Durkheim, having established the autonomy of social facts using the criterion of externality, in effect employed just such a criterion to establish their reality, in invoking his other criterion of constraint:

> I am not obliged to speak French with my fellow-countrymen nor to use the legal currency, but I cannot possibly do otherwise. If I tried to escape this necessity, my attempts would fail miserably. As an industrialist, I am free to apply the technical methods of former centuries; but by doing so I should invite certain ruin. Even when I free myself from these rules and violate them successfully, I am always compelled to struggle with them. When finally overcome, they make their constraining power felt by the resistance they offer.'[39]

Durkheim is saying in effect that but for the range of social facts particularly sequences of sounds, movements of bodies etc. would not occur. Of course one must insist, against Durkheim, that the range of social facts depends upon the intentional activity of men. The individualist truth that people are the only moving forces in history—in the sense that nothing happens behind their backs, that is, everyting that happens, happens in and through their actions—must be retained. Moreover one must conceive social structures as in principle enabling, and not just coercive. Nevertheless in employing a causal criterion to establish the reality of social facts, Durkheim observed perfectly proper scientific practice.[40] Though it must be noticed that we are here dealing with a most peculiar kind of entity: a structure irreducible to, but present only in, its effects.

What is the connection between the transformational model of social activity developed in the previous section and the relational conception of the subject matter of sociology advanced in the third section. The relational conception does not of course deny that factories and books are social forms. But it maintains that their being *social*, as distinct from (or rather in addition to) material, objects consists only in the relationships between persons or between such relationships and nature that such objects causally presuppose or entail. The *social* conditions for the structures that govern the substantive activities of transformation in which men engage (and which constitute the immediate explanation of these activities) can thus only be relations of various kinds: between people and each other, their products, their activities, nature and themselves. If social activity is to be given a social explanation it is in this nexus that it must be found. It is thus in the enduring relations presupposed by, rather than the actual complex motley of particular social forms, that on this conception, sociology's distinctive theoretical interest lies.

Marx combined a relational conception of social science and a transformational model of social activities with the additional premiss – of historical materialism – that it is material production that is ultimately determining of the rest of social life.[41] Now, as is well known, although it can be established *a priori* that material production is a necessary condition for social life, it cannot be established *a priori* that it is an ultimately determining one. And so like any other fundamental metaphysical blueprint or paradigm in science historical materialism can only be justified by its fruitfulness in generating research programmes capable of yielding sequences of theories, progressively richer in explanatory power. Not the least of the problems facing historical materialism is that, although progress has been made in particular areas of explanation, the blueprint itself still awaits adequate articulation. (One has only to think of the problem of reconciling the thesis of the relative autonomy of the superstructures with that of determination in the last instance by the base[42] to be reminded of this.)

The limits of naturalism

How, given that societies exist, and have the kinds of properties that they do, might they become possible objects of knowledge for us?

The major ontological limits on the possibility of naturalism, turning on the activity-, concept-, and space-time-dependence of social structures, have already been isolated. Before considering how social scientific knowledge is possible, despite or as I shall try to show because of these features, I want to consider two other kinds of limit on naturalism, which I shall characterize as epistemological and relational respectively.

Society, as an object of inquiry, is necessarily 'theoretical' in the sense that, like a magnetic field, it is necessarily unperceivable; so that it cannot be empirically identified independently of its effects, that is it can only be known, not shown, to exist. However in this respect it is not differentiated from many objects of natural scientific inquiry. What does differentiate it is that society not only cannot be empirically identified independently of its effects, but it does not *exist* independently of them either. But, however strange this is from an ontological point of view,[43] it raises no special epistemological difficulties.

The chief epistemological limit on naturalism is not raised by the necessarily unperceivable character of the objects of social scientific investigation, but by the fact that they only manifest themselves in 'open systems'; that is in systems where invariant empirical regularities do not obtain. Now the real methodological import of this point must be distinguished most carefully from its significance for the doctrines of received philosophy of science. It is as easy to exaggerate the former, as to underestimate the latter. For, as I have shown in detail elsewhere,[44] practically all the theories of orthodox philosophy of science, and the methodological directives they secrete, presuppose closed systems. Because of this, they are totally inapplicable to the social sciences—which is not of course to say that the attempt cannot be made to apply them, with disastrous results. Humeian theories of causality and law, deductive—nomological and statistical models of explanation, inductivist theories of scientific development and criteria of confirmation, and Popperian theories of scientific rationality and criteria of falsification, together with the hermeneutical contrasts parasitic upon them, must all be totally discarded. The only concern of social science with them is as objects of substantive explanation.

The real methodological import of the absence of spontaneously occurring, and the impossibility of artificially creating, closed systems is strictly limited: it is that the social sciences are denied, in principle, decisive test situations for their theories. This means that the criteria for the rational confirmation and rejection of theories in social science *cannot be predictive*, and so must be *exclusively explanatory*. Particularly important here will be the capacity of a theory to be developed in a non-*ad hoc* way so as to situate, and preferably explain, without strain, a possibility, once (and perhaps even before) it is realized, when it could never, given the openness of the social world, have predicted it. It should be stressed that this difference has in itself no ontological significance whatsoever. It does not affect the form of laws, which in natural science too must be analysed as tendencies; only the form of our knowledge of them. Because the mode of application of laws is the same in open and closed systems alike,[45] the mode of application of laws is the same in society as in nature. And although the necessity to rely exclusively on explanatory criteria *may* affect the subjective confidence with which one holds social scientific theories, if one has *independently* validated claims to social scientific knowledge (on explanatory criteria) then one is just as warranted in applying knowledge as in natural science. Or rather, given that the problem is not typically whether or not to apply some theory, T, to the world, but rather *which* out of two or more theories, T, T′, etc. to apply, the degree of the preference for one theory over another will not be affected by a limitation on the grounds with which that preference must be justified.

In addition to allowing (relatively)[46] decisive test situations, experimental activity in the natural sciences, in enabling access to the otherwise latent structures of nature, may provide an invaluable component of the process of scientific discovery that the social sciences, in this respect, will be denied. However, the discussion of the relational and ontological limits will generate an analogue and a compensator respectively for this role in discovery.

The chief relational difference is that the social sciences are part of their own field of inquiry, in principle susceptible to explanation in terms of the concepts and laws of the explanatory theories they employ; so that it is *internal* with respect to its subject matter in a way in which natural science is not. This qualifies the sense in which the objects of social scientific investigation can be said to be intransitive, that is exist and act independently of it. For it is possible and indeed likely, given the internal complexity and interdependence of social activities, that its objects do not exist independently of, and may be causally affected by, social science; just as one might expect that social science is affected or conditioned by developments in, as it patently cannot exist independently of, the rest of society. So far the argument has turned merely on the possibility of a relatively undifferentiated society/social science link. But the case for such a link may be strengthened by noting that just as a social science without a society is impossible, so a society without some kind of scientific, proto-scientific, or ideological theory of itself is inconceivable (even if it consists merely in the conceptions that the agents have of what they are doing in their activity). Now if one denotes the proto-scientific set of ideas P, then the transformational model of social activity applied to the activity of knowledge-production would suggest that social scientific theory, T, requiring cognitive resources is produced, at least in part, by the transformation of P. The hypothesis under consideration is that this transformation will be vitally affected by developments in the rest of society, S.

It might be conjectured that in periods of transition or crisis generative structures, formerly opaque, become more visible to men.[47] And that this, though it never yields the epistemic possibilities of a closure, does provide a partial analogue to the role that experimental activity plays in natural science. The social conditions for the production and emergence of a social scientific theory must of course be distinguished from the conditions for its subsequent development and (though there are evident connections between the two) from the conditions for its wider societal influence or assent.[48] Thus it is surely no accident that Marxism was born in the 1840s or stunted in the East under Stalin and in the West during the Cold War and post-war boom. Or that sociology, in the narrow sense, was the fruit of the two decades before the First World War.[49]

It should be noted that because social systems are open historicism (in the sense of deductively justified prediction) is untenable. Moreover, because of the historical (transformational) character of social systems, qualitatively new developments in society will be occurring which social scientific theory cannot be expected to anticipate. Hence for ontological, as distinct from purely epistemological, reasons, social scientific, unlike natural scientific, theory is *necessarily* incomplete. Moreover, as the possibilities inherent in a new social development will often only become apparent long after the development itself, and as each new development is, in a sense, a product of a previous one, one can see why it is that history must be continually rewritten. There is a relational tie between the development of the object of knowledge and the development of knowledge that any adequate theory of social science, and methodology of social scientific research programmes, must take account of. In particular, Lakatosian judgments about the progressive or degenerating nature of research programmes[50] in the social sciences cannot be made in isolation from judgments about factors in the rest of society, S, conditioning work in particular programmes.

Once a hypothesis of a causal mechanism has been produced in social science it can then be tested quite *empirically*, though exclusively by reference to its explanatory power. But I have so far said nothing about how the hypothesis of the generative mechanism is produced, or indeed about what its status is. It is to these questions that I now turn.

In considering theory construction in the social sciences it should be borne in mind that the putative social scientist would, in the absence of some prior theory, be faced with an inchoate mass of social phenomena, which he would somehow have to sort out and define. In systems, like social ones, which are necessarily open, the problem of constituting an appropriate (that is explanatorily significant) object of inquiry becomes particularly acute. Fortunately most of the phenomena with which the social scientist has to deal will already be identified, thanks to the *concept-dependent* nature of social activities, under certain descriptions. In principle the descriptions or nominal definitions of social activities that form the transitive objects of social scientific theory may be those of the agents concerned or theoretical redescriptions of them. The first step in the transformation P → T will thus be an attempt at a real definition of a form of social life that has already been identified under a particular description. Note that in the absence of such a definition, and failing a closure, any hypothesis of a causal mechanism is bound to be more or less arbitrary. Thus in social science attempts at real definitions will in general precede rather than follow successful causal hypotheses – though in both cases they can only be justified empirically, viz. by the revealed explanatory power of the hypotheses that can be derived from them.

The problem, then, is shifted from that of how to establish a non-arbitrary procedure for generating causal hypotheses to that of how to establish a non-arbitrary procedure for generating real definitions. And here a second differentiating feature of the subject matter of the social sciences should be recalled – the *activity-dependent* nature of social structures, viz. that the mechanisms at work in society exist only in virtue of their effects. In this respect society is quite distinct from other objects of scientific knowledge. But note that, in this, it is analogous to the objects of philosophical knowledge. For just as the objects of philosophical knowledge do not exist as objects of a world apart from the objects of scientific knowledge, so social structures do not exist apart from their effects. So I suggest that in principle as philosophical discourse stands to scientific discourse, so a discourse about society stands to a discourse about its effects. Moreover, in both cases one is dealing with conceptualized activities, whose conditions of possibility or presuppositions the second order discourse seeks to explicate. However, there are also important differences. For in social scientific discourse one is concerned not to isolate the general conditions of knowledge as such, but the particular mechanisms and relations at work in some identified sphere of social life. Moreover, its conclusions will be historical, not formal; and subject to empirical test, as well as to various *a priori* controls.[51]

It is here that the hermeneutical tradition, in highlighting what may be called the conceptual moment in social scientific work, has made a real contribution. But it makes two mistakes. Its continuing commitment to the ontology of empirical realism prevents it from seeing (1) that the conditions for the phenomena, namely social activities as conceptualized in experience, may be *real*; and (2) that the phenomena themselves may be *false* or in an important sense inadequate.

Thus what has been established, by conceptual analysis, as necessary for the phenomena may consist precisely in that extra-conceptual reality which consists in the real relations and processes in which people stand to each other and nature, of which they may or may not be aware; which is really generative of social life and yet unavailable to direct inspection by the senses. Moreover, such a transcendental analysis in social science in showing the historical conditions under which a set of categories may be validly applied *ipso facto* shows the conditions under which they may not be applied. This makes possible a second-order critique of consciousness, best exemplified perhaps by Marx's analysis of commodity fetishism.[52] Value relations, it will be remembered, for Marx, are real but they are historically specific social realities. And fetishism consists in their transformation in thought into the natural, and so ahistorical, qualities of things. But as Norman Geras has pointed out,[53] Marx employed another concept of mystification. This is best exemplified by his treatment of the wage form, in which the value of labour power is transformed into the value of labour. This Marx declares to be an expression 'as imaginary as the value of the earth', 'as irrational as a yellow logarithm'.[54] Here he engages in what one may call a first-order critique of consciousness – in which, to put it bluntly, he identifies the phenomena themselves as false; or, more formally, shows that a certain set of categories are not properly applicable to experience at all. Thus, contrary to what is implied in the transcendental idealist tradition, the transformation P → T both (1) isolates real but non-empirical conditions and (2) consists essentially, as critique, in two types of conceptual criticism and change.

Now the appellation 'ideology' to the set of ideas P is only justified if their *necessity* can be demonstrated; that is if they can be explained, as well as criticized.[55] This involves something more than just being able to say that the beliefs concerned are false (or superficial) and being able to say why they are false or superficial, which normally entails of course having a superior explanation for the phenomenon in question. It involves, in addition, being able to give an account of the *reason* why the false or superficial beliefs are *held* – a mode of explanation clearly without parallel in the natural sciences. For beliefs, whether about society or nature, are clearly social objects.

Once this step is taken then conceptual criticism and change passes over into social criticism and change. For, in a possibility unique to social science, the object that renders illusory beliefs necessary comes, at least in the absence of any overriding considerations, to be criticized in being explained. So that the point now becomes, *ceteris paribus*, to change it. In the full development of the concept of ideology, theory fuses into practice, as facts about values, mediated by theories about facts, are transformed into values about facts.[56] The rule of value-neutrality, the last shibboleth of the philosophy of social science, collapses, when we come to see that values themselves can be false.

To sum up, then, society is not given in, but presupposed by, experience. But it is precisely its peculiar ontological status, its transcendentally real character, that makes it a possible object of knowledge for us. Such knowledge is non-natural but still scientific.

As for the law-like statements of the social sciences, they designate tendencies operating at a single level of the social structure only. Because they are defined only for one relatively autonomous component of the social structure and because they act in systems that are always open, they designate tendencies (such as for the rates of profit on capitalist enterprises to be equalized) which may never be manifested. But which are nevertheless essential to the understanding and the changing of, just because they are really productive of, the different forms of social life.

As for society itself it is not, as the positivists would have it, a mass of separable events and sequences. Nor is it constituted, as a rival school would have it, by the momentary meanings that we attach to our physiological states. Rather it is a complex and causally efficacious whole – a totality, whose concept must be constructed in theory, and which is being continually transformed in practice. As an object of study, it cannot be read straight off the empirical world. But neither can it be reconstructed from our subjective experiences. But, though positivism would have had us forget it, that much at least is the case with the objects of study in natural science too.

Notes

1   See P. Winch, *The Idea of a Social Science* (London 1958) esp. pp. 114–15.
2   *Ibid*, esp. pp. 108, 124–5.
3   Especially R. Harré, *The Principles of Scientific Thinking* (London 1970); R. Harré & E. H. Madden, *Causal Powers* (Oxford 1975); and R. Bhaskar, *A Realist Theory of Science*, 2nd edn. (Hassocks, and New Jersey 1978). See R. Keat, 'Positivism, naturalism and anti-naturalism in the social sciences', *Journal for the Theory of Social Behaviour*, I. 1971, pp. 3–17; R. Harre and P. F. Secord, *The Explanation of Social Behaviour* (Oxford 1972); and R. Keat and J. Urry, *Social Theory as Science* (London 1975).
4   See my *A Realist Theory of Science*, especially chs. 1 and 2.
5   *Ibid*, ch. 2, sec. 4.
6   *Loc. cit.*
7   See R. Harré, *Principles of Scientific Thinking*, especially ch. 2; and M. Hesse, *Models and Analogies in Science* (Indianapolis 1966), especially ch. 1.
8   See N. R. Hanson, *Patterns of Discovery* (Cambridge 1965), especially pp. 85ff.
9   See *A Realist Theory of Science*, p. 182.
10   See K. R. Popper, *The Open Society and its Enemies*, II (London 1962), p. 98.
11   I. Jarvie, *Universities and Left Review* (1959), p. 57.
12   J. W. N. Watkins, 'Historical explanation in the social sciences', *British Journal of the Philosophy of Science*, VIII (1957), reprinted as 'Methodological individualism and social tendencies', *Readings in the Philosophy of the Social Sciences*, M. Brodbeck (ed.) (New York 1968), p. 271.
13   *Loc. cit.*
14   J. W. N. Watkins 'Ideal types and historical explanation', *British Journal of the Philosophy of Science*, III (1952); reprinted in *The Philosophy of Social Explanation*, A. Ryan (ed.) (Oxford 1973), p. 88.
15   See A. Danto, *Analytical Philosophy of History* (Cambridge 1965), ch. 12, and S. Lukes, 'Methodological individualism reconsidered', *British Journal of Sociology*, XIX (1968), reprinted in A. Ryan, *op cit.*
16   J.W.N. Watkins, 'Ideal types', p. 91 and 'Methodological individualism', p. 273.
17   *Ibid*, p. 278.
18   D. Hume, *A. Treatise on Human Nature*, L. A. Selby-Bigge (ed.) (Oxford 1968), p. 415.
19   D. Hume, *Essays Moral and Political*, vol. II, T. H. Green and T. H. Grose (ed.) (London 1875), p. 68.

20 See S. Kotarbinski, 'Praxiology', *Essays in honour of O. Lange* (Warsaw 1965).

21 J. P. Sartre, *Critique of Dialectical Reason* (London 1976), bk. 2, ch. 1 and bk. 1, ch. 4.

22 There are, of course, non-, and even anti-individualist tendencies in Weber's thought [see for example R. Aron, *Philosophie Critique de l'histoire* (Paris 1969)]; just as there are non-, and (especially in *The Elementary Forms of Religious Life*) anti-positivist strains in Durkheim's [see for example R. Horton 'Lévy-Bruhl, Durkheim and the Scientific Revolution', *Modes of Thought*, R. Finnegan and R. Horton (eds.)(London 1973)].

23 See R. Keat and J. Urry, *op. cit.*, ch. 5, and B. Ollman, *Alienation* (Cambridge 1971), esp. chs. 2 and 3 respectively.

24 See especially P. Berger and Pullberg 'Reification and the sociological critique of consciousness', *New Left Review*, XXXV (1966), and P. Berger and T. Luckman, *The Social Construction of Reality* (London 1967).

25 'Reification', pp. 62–3.

26 *Ibid*, p. 63.

27 *Loc. cit.*

28 E. Durkheim, *The Rules of Sociological Method* (New York 1964), p. 2.

29 'Reification', p. 60.

30 *Ibid*, p. 61.

31 *Ibid*, p. 60.

32 *Rules of Sociological Method*, pp. 1–2.

33 This is of course the fundamental insight of the hermeneutical tradition in the philosophy of social science. See W. Outhwaite, *Understanding Social Life* (London 1975).

34 Marx, perhaps, comes closest to articulating his conception of history: 'History is nothing but the succession of the separate generations, each of which exploits the materials, the capital the productive forces handed down to it by all proceeding generations, and thus, on the one hand continues the traditional activity in completely changed circumstances and, on the other, modifies the old circumstances with a completely changed activity', K. Marx and F. Engels, *The German Ideology* (London 1965), p. 66.

35 See Lévi-Strauss, *The Savage Mind* (London 1966), ch. 1.

36 The internal complexity and interdependence of social structures does not mark a *necessary* difference with natural structures.

37 See R. Harré and P. F. Secord, *op. cit.*, esp. ch. 5.

38 *A Realist Theory of Science*, p. 113. See also M. Polanyi, *The Tacit Dimension* (London 1967), ch. 2.

39 *Rules of Sociological Method*, p. 2.

40 Although Durkheim used a causal criterion to establish the reality of social facts on a collectivist conception of sociology, the same criterion can be used to establish their reality on a relational one. (There is no special difficulty, as for example the concept of spin in physics shows, in ascribing reality to relations on a causal criterion).

41 According to Marx, men 'begin to distinguish themselves from animals as soon as they begin to *produce* their means of subsistence', *The German Ideology*, p. 31.

The first premiss of all human existence and therefore of all history [is] the premiss . . . that men must be in a position to live in order to be able to "make history". But life involves before anything eating and drinking, a habitation, clothing and many other things. The first historical act is thus the production of the means to satisfy these needs, the production of material life itself, *ibid.*, p. 39.

('The first historical act' must of course be understood in an analytical, not chronological, sense.) See also: 'In all forms of society it is a determinate production and its relations which assign every other production and its relations their rank and influence. It is a general illumination in which all other colours are plunged and which modifies their specific tonalities. It is a special ether which defines the specific gravity of everything found within it', K. Marx, *Grundrisse* (Harmondsworth 1973), p. 107.

42 The problem for marxism has always been to find a way of avoiding both economic (or worse technological) reductionism and historical eclecticism, so that it does actually generate some substantive historiographical propositions. It is a problem of which both Marx and Engels were aware. Thus as Engels was at pains to stress:

'According to the materialist conception of history, the economy is the ultimately determining element in history. [But] if someone twists this into saying that it is the *only* determining [one], he transforms this proposition into a meaningless, abstract, senseless phrase. The economic situation is the basis, but the various elements of the superstructure . . . also exercise their influence upon the course of events . . . and in many cases preponderate in determining their form. There is an interaction of all these elements in which, amid the endless host of accidents, the economic movement finally asserts itself as necessary.' [F. Engels, Letter to J. Bloch, 21 September 1890, *Marx – Engels Selected Works*, II, Lawrence & Wishart (London 1968), p. 692.)].

But how are we to conceptualize this ultimate necessity? Marx provides a clue. Replying to an objection he concedes that 'the mode of production of material life dominates the development of social, political and intellectual life generally . . . is very true for our time, in which material interests preponderate, but not for the middle ages, in which Catholicism, nor for Athens or Rome, where politics, reigned supreme'. But Marx contends 'this much [also] is clear. That the middle ages could not live on Catholicism, nor the Ancient World on Politics [alone]. On the contrary, it is the economic conditions of the time that explains why here politics and there Catholicism played the chief part.' [K. Marx, *Capital*, I (London 1965), p. 81n.] Althusser has attempted to theorize this insight by saying that it is the economy that *determines* which relatively autonomous structure in the social totality is the *dominant* one. [See L. Althusser, *For Marx* (London 1969), and L. Althusser and E. Balibar, *Reading Capital* (London 1970)].

43   But is the notion of a 'field' that exists only in virtue of its effects any stranger, or *prima facie* more absurd, than the combination of principles of wave and particle mechanics in elementary micro-physics, now reckoned a common-place?

44   *A Realist Theory of Science*, Appendix to ch. 2.

45   *Ibid*, ch. 2, sec. 4.

46   See P. Duhem, *The Aim and Structure of Physical Theory* (New York 1962), pp. 180–90.

47   If true, this would have an analogue in the domain of social psychology in the conscious technique of 'Garfinkelling' [see for example H. Garfinkel, *Essays in Ethnomethodology* (New Jersey 1967)], and perhaps in the role played by psychopathology in the development of a general psychology.

48   Consider, for example, the way in which the mass unemployment of the 1930s not only provided the theoretical dynamo for the Keynesian innovation, but facilitated its ready acceptance by the relevant scientific community.

49   See for example S. Giddens, *Capitalism and Modern Theory* (Cambridge 1971), Postscript; and G. Therborn, *Science, Class and Society* (London 1976), ch. 5, pt. 3.

50   See for example I. Lakatos 'Falsification and the methodology of scientific research programmes', *Criticism and the Growth of Knowledge* (eds.) I. Lakatos and A. Musgrave. (Cambridge 1970).

51   Thus the transformational model of social activity implies that it is a necessary condition for any adequate theory of a social system that the theory be capable of showing how the system reproduces or transforms itself. *A priori* considerations of this sort can be used to criticize particular social theories. See, for example, M. Hollis and E. Nell, *Rational Economic Man* (Cambridge 1975), especially ch. 8 for a criticism of neo-classical economic theory along these lines.

52   K. Marx, *Capital*, I, ch. 1.

53   N. Geras, 'Essence and appearance: aspects of fetishism in Marx's *Capital*', *New Left Review*, 65 (1971), reprinted as 'Marx and the critique of political economy', *Ideology in Social Science*, R. Blackburn (ed.) (London 1972), p. 291.

54   See *Capital*, I, p. 537 and *Capital*, III, p. 798 respectively.

55   N. Geras, *op. cit.*, and J. Mepham, 'The theory of ideology in *Capital*', *Radical Philosophy*, II (1972) (Reprinted in this volume).

56   C. Taylor 'Neutrality in political science', *Philosophy, Politics and* 3rd series, P. Laslett and W. Runciman (eds.), reprinted in A. Ryan *op. cit.*, shows clearly how theories (or 'explanatory frameworks') do in fact secrete values. Unfortunately, however, by not specifying

any criterion for choosing between theories, he leaves himself open to the interpretation that one should choose that theory that most satisfies our conception of what 'fulfils human needs, wants and purposes' (p. 161); rather than that theory which, *just because it is explanatorily most adequate*, and capable *inter alia* of explaining illusory beliefs about the social world, best allows us to situate the possibilities of change in the value-direction that the theory indicates. Taylor thus merely displaces, rather than transcends, the traditional fact/value dichotomy.

The Theory of Ideology in Capital
JOHN MEPHAM

'There must be some way out of here'
Said the joker to the thief
'There's too much confusion
I can't get no relief'

(Dylan)

Where do incorrect ideas come from?
IN *What is to be Done?* Lenin argues that 'the spontaneous
development of the working-class movement leads to its
subordination to bourgeois ideology'.[1] It is the necessity of
going beyond the spontaneous development of the movement
that is the basis of his argument for a three-fold struggle,
theoretical, political and economic. It is in the same context
that he makes the famous statement that 'without revolutionary theory there can be no revolutionary movement'.[2]
What are the epistemological bases of these interconnected
necessities, the spontaneous dominance of bourgeois ideology
and the need for theory? Standing behind such analyses
there must be a theory of the conditions for the production
of knowledge and of effective practice and also a theory of
the production of mystification. In *What is to be Done?*,
which is not intended as a work on the theory of knowledge,
Lenin only offers a passing remark about the origins of
mystification.

> But why, the reader will ask, does the spontaneous movement, the
> movement along the line of least resistance, lead to the domination
> of bourgeois ideology? For the simple reason that bourgeois ideology
> is far older in origin than socialist ideology, that it is more fully
> developed, and that it has at its disposal immeasurably more means
> of dissemination.[3]

Now I think that this statement is, not surprisingly given its context, incomplete, and is open to misinterpretation. It may suggest a view that is very common but which is, in my opinion, fundamentally mistaken. This view, which is an ideology of ideology, is that the dominance of bourgeois ideology has its basis in the dominance of the bourgeoisie as a class only in the sense that this dominance as a class allows the bourgeoisie to have a monopoly on the production and dissemination of ideas. Thus, from the point of view of the workers ideas have their origin in the means of the dissemination of ideas produced originally elsewhere. Ideas are transmitted, via cultural and educational institutions, public communications systems and so on, into the otherwise empty minds of the working class. It could be that conditions in midtwentieth-century bourgeois society are such as to spontaneously suggest this view. There is no doubt that midtwentieth-century capitalism does generate a formidable semic pollution to a degree and of kinds quite unimaginable one hundred or even fifty years ago. The very forms and modern technological means of the production and dissemination of ideas (the 'advertising industry', the 'public' television and radio systems, political campaigns designed around the production of 'images' of politicians etc., etc.) do seem to suggest a social division between the producers of ideas (advertising copy writers, press agents, speech writers etc.) and the consumers of ideas ('the public').[4] And some writers who have attempted to diagnose our contemporary condition ('one-dimensional man') do, perhaps because of this, stumble sometimes into the error of mislocating the source of mystification in the way defined above. Marcuse, for example, in his essay 'Repressive Tolerance' tends to identify the conditions under which people live and think, and which thereby determine *what* they think, with the 'prevailing indoctrination' by the 'media', advertisements and so on, to which they are exposed. He says 'The people exposed to this impartiality are no *tabulae rasae*, they are indoctrinated by the conditions under which they live and think and which they do not transcend. To enable them to become autonomous, to find by themselves what is true and what is false for man in the existing society, they would have to be freed from the prevailing indoctrination ... ' And 'different opinions and "philosophies" can no longer compete peacefully for adherence and persuasion on rational grounds: the "market-place of ideas" is organized and delimited by those who determine the national and the individual interest'.[5] Perhaps if it were only Marcuse who made this mistake it would not deserve so much emphasis here. I believe, however, that it is a mistake very commonly made by, for example, the students that I teach, and it is perhaps what Marx would call a 'natural and spontaneous mode of thought' in contemporary capitalist society. If this is so then this view is self-refuting because it would itself be ideology which has its origins in something other than the indoctrination which it identifies as the origins of ideology.

In what follows I do not, of course, intend to deny for one moment that the bourgeoisie *do* control the means for the dissemination of ideas in Lenin's sense, nor that they do use this control as a powerful weapon in the defence of their class-interests. But my view is that the bourgeois class is the producer of ideas only in the sense that sleep is the producer of dreams. To say that the bourgeoisie produces ideas is to ignore the conditions that make this possible, to ignore that which determines *which* ideas are thus produced, and to conceal the real nature and origins of ideology. It is not the bourgeois *class* that produces ideas but bourgeois *society*. And the effective dissemination of ideas is only possible because, or to the extent that, the ideas thus disseminated are ideas which, for quite different reasons, do have a sufficient degree of effectiveness both in rendering social reality intelligible and in guiding practice within it for them to be apparently acceptable. It is the relation between ideology and reality that is the key to its dominance. To show this one would have to explore the relation between the 'representations in mens' brains' and the reality of which these are representations both as a cognitive and as a practical relation. In what follows I will for the most part be concerned with the cognitive aspect of this relation.

The Theory of Ideology in The German Ideology
The obvious place to begin is with those passages in *The German Ideology* in which Marx discusses the epistemology

of mystification. But my claim will be that, in fact, Marx has not, in such early works on which discussions of ideology are usually based, achieved a clear theoretical position on the origin of ideology, and that the metaphors in terms of which he discusses the problem have to be drastically modified in the light of what he says in his later works. I claim that on this epistemological question of the origin of incorrect ideas *Capital* is a great advance on *The German Ideology*.

In a familiar and typical passage from *The German Ideology* Marx says:

> If in all ideology men and their circumstances appear upside down as in a *camera obscura*, this phenomenon arises just as much from their historical life process as the inversion of objects on the retina does from their physical life process. . . . We set out from real, active men, and on the basis of their real life process we demonstrate the development of the ideological reflexes and echoes of this life process. The phantoms formed in the human brain are also, necessarily, sublimates of their material life process, which is empirically verifiable and bound to material premises. . . . [6]

Now this is not a clear statement. Marx is here struggling to discover an adequate language and the result is a series of metaphors which are the symptoms of his failure (not that metaphors as such are a symptom of failure in philosophy. Here it is the profusion of them which suggests that none of them alone satisfies the author – *camera obscura*, reflexes, echoes, phantoms, sublimates . . .). Also the passage is open to many different interpretations. Perhaps most unfortunately the words 'empirically verifiable' and 'material premises' taken together with the word 'phantom' suggest a positivist interpretation. This would be that ideology arises from the tendency to be taken in by phantoms in such a way that the victim simply overlooks or is distracted from 'empirically verifiable facts' that would otherwise be obvious and clear.

As a way of focusing later on the model of relations involved in the production of ideology which I will extract from *Capital* it will be useful at this point to make explicit some of the features involved in the use of the *camera obscura* metaphor. This metaphor involves the following representations of the relations between reality and ideas.

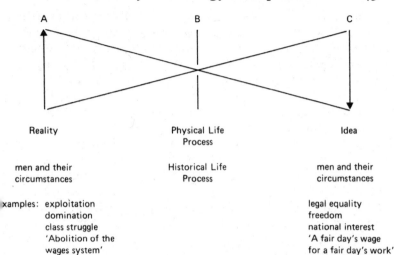

A	B	C
Reality	Physical Life Process	Idea
men and their circumstances	Historical Life Process	men and their circumstances

Examples: exploitation
domination
class struggle
'Abolition of the
wages system'

legal equality
freedom
national interest
'A fair day's wage
for a fair day's work'

This metaphor suggests that in the production of ideology there are the following aspects:

(1) Three independent entities: the real object A, the representation C, and the mediating entity (light) B which effects the production of the latter from the former. Each idea is the distorted representation of some one 'thing' in reality to which it corresponds in a one-to-one manner.

(2) The relation between A and C is one of inversion. The transformation A to C preserves all internal relations.

(3) The metaphor not only suggests the independence of the entity reflected, A, (it does not need C in order to exist) and denies the independence of C (ideas are not themselves among the conditions for the production of ideas), but also suggests that representations are in some sense 'mere illusions' (an epistemological thesis) and 'mere epiphenomena' or 'phantoms' (an ontological thesis).

It seems to follow that they (the representations) can therefore have no element of either truth or practical effectiveness. These suggestions amount to a thesis of crude materialism with which Marx certainly disagreed. Why then is Marx so fascinated with this metaphor which is very frequent throughout his work and which has led to gross misinterpretations of his views?

The structure of ideology and its relation to reality
I shall now state three theses concerning the structure of

ideology and its relation to reality. These are stated in such a way as to make it clear that they are different from views on ideology mentioned above. I shall in following sections show how these theses amount to a part of a theory of ideology that is implicit in *Capital*.

Thesis 1. Ideology is structured discourse. It is, directly or indirectly, based on or generated by a set of mutually inter-dependent categories. The view that ideology is made up of *ideas* is itself misleading to the extent that this has been taken in philosophy to suggest that the units of which ideology is composed, or out of which it is constructed, are independent of one another, and that they can be traced back to atomistic ideas which are derived from reality 'one at a time', or on a one-to-one basis (as for example in the relation A to C in the *camera obscura* metaphor). One cannot understand ideological concepts or ideological propositions as standing in some such one-to-one relation with non-ideological, non-distorted, factual or scientific concepts, propositions or facts. The translation of ideology (or manifest text) into the true, under-lying (latent) text cannot be performed on a word-to-word or proposition-to-proposition basis. The 'true text' is recon-structed not by a process of piecemeal decoding but by the identification of the generative set of ideological categories and its replacement by a different set. This different set will be differently constituted in its internal relations. And one must discover the transformational mechanism whereby the distorted matrix is, in the historical life process substituted for the undistorted one.

Thesis 2. The relation between reality and ideology (which produces 'inversion') is the cognitive relation. That is to say that mystification has its basis in the perception of the apparently intelligible order of social reality by a process of 'misrecognition'. An implication of this second thesis is that ideology does not derive fundamentally from the intention to deceive others, from self-deception, or in the perversion of cognition by its being infected with values (for example the value of self- or class-interests). Nor does ideology derive fundamentally from the cognitive function being overwhelmed by non-cognitive functions such as the emotions, feelings or passions. I am not denying that ideology does have the effect of, or does constitute mystification or deception, and that it does function as a defence of class-interests, and does have the result that what *appears* to be objective, positive, scientific discourse is not in fact 'value-free'.

I will try to clarify this second thesis and its implications by reference to some analogies. This will also help to locate this discussion in a broader context. I am thinking of the problem of ideology in relation to the general questions, 'What are the conditions for the production of knowledge and what are the conditions for the production of various systems of mystificatory belief?'. These questions have been raised not only in relation to ideology but also, for example, in relation to the history of science and to the problem of myth in anthropology.[7] As one aspect (but only one; there are many others) of such enquiries progress has been achieved I think by the rediscovery, paradoxical as it may seem, of the cognitive basis of some systems of mystificatory belief. The history of science makes great strides to the extent that it rejects the view that 'pre-scientific' systems of belief and practice such as alchemy or natural magic resulted from simple lack of interest in the empirical facts, or from ignorance of the importance of empirical study, or from simple empirical mistakes or oversights; and also rejects the view that such systems were essentially the result of enterprises that were overwhelmed entirely by non-cognitive subjective forces (for example greed or 'mysticism'). One might claim in fact that such systems were possible by virtue of the fact that they were too firmly established on the basis of the 'immediately perceivable' forms of empirical reality (such as for example the occurrence of the transformation of apparently elemental substances, systems of perceivable relations of analogy, sympathy and antipathy and so on).[8] Similarly anthropological study of myth has progressed to the extent that it has refused the ethnocentric prejudice that myth is pure 'superstition' satisfying only affective demands or that it is infantile proto-science which paid insufficient attention to detailed empirical facts. This is clearly one of the main themes of Lévi-Strauss in *La Pensée Sauvage*. Elsewhere Lévi-Strauss identifies the main mistake in the work of Lévi-Bruhl by saying that 'he denied to "primitive mentality" the cognitive character which he had initially conceded to it, and cast it back entirely into the realm of affectivity'.[9]

Thesis 3. Ideology arises from the opacity of reality, where the opacity of reality is the fact that the forms in which reality 'presents itself' to men, or the forms of its appearance, conceal those real relations which themselves produce the appearances. This thesis involves the introduction of the concepts *phenomenal form*, *real relation* and *opacity*. It is stated explicitly by Marx, for example in vol. I, ch. 19, which is called 'The Transformation of the Value of Labour-Power into Wages'. 'Value of Labour-Power' is the name of a real relation, and 'Wages' (or the wage-form) is a phenomenal form. The selling of the commodity labour-power is the real relation of exchange which is transformed, in experience, into the mystifying phenomenal form Wages or wage-contract, thus disguising the real nature of the social relations involved in transactions between capitalist and labourer in bourgeois society. In political economy the mystified form 'value of labour' (as distinct from the 'value of labour-power') is identified with wages.[10]

> Hence, we may understand the decisive importance of the trans-formation of value and price of labour-power into the form of wages, or into the value and price of labour itself. This phenomenal form, which makes the actual relation invisible, and, indeed, shows the direct opposite of that relation, forms the basis of all the juridical notions of both labourer and capitalist, of all the mystifications of the capitalist mode of production, of all its illusions as to liberty, of all the apologetic shifts of the vulgar economists. (p. 540)

This third thesis involves an important aspect of Marx's epistemology, namely his distinction between 'phenomenal forms' (or appearances) and 'real relations' as developed in *Capital* in the context of a critique of the categories of political economy. Marx himself thought his most fundamental theoretical break-through the discovery of the true concept of surplus-value which enabled him to penetrate in a rigorous way to the secret and hidden realities of capitalism. It is this theoretical advance that also allows Marx to make a decisive move beyond the ambiguities of his earlier remarks on ideology. Marx's claim is then that it is the importance of the phenomenal forms that they render invisible real relations and hence give rise to bourgeois ideology. Here is another example of Marx's use of these concepts.

> ... in respect to the *phenomenal form*, 'value and price of labour', or 'wages', as contrasted with the *essential relation* manifested therein, viz. the value and price of labour-power, the same difference holds in respect to all *phenomena* and their *hidden substratum*. The former *appear directly and spontaneously* as current modes of thought; the latter must first be discovered by science. Classical Political Economy nearly touches the *true relation of things*, without, however, consciously formulating it. This it cannot so long as it sticks in its bourgeois skin. (p. 542) (My emphases)

Notice that here Marx is making a *general* point ('the same difference holds in respect to all phenomena and their hidden substratum'), and is not limiting his remarks to this particular categorical transformation and mystification. And second it should be noted that Marx is here providing us with an answer to the question with which we started 'Why does the spontaneous movement lead to the domination of bourgeois ideology?', namely that phenomenal forms appear 'directly and spontaneously as current modes of thought'.

These three theses stated in this section can be summed up in a remark by Henri Lefebvre,[11]

> Social reality, that is interacting human individuals and groups, produces *appearances* which are something more and else than mere illusions. Such appearances are the modes in which human activities manifest themselves within the whole they constitute at any given moment – call them modalities of consciousness. They have far greater consistency, let alone coherence, than mere illusions or ordinary lies. Appearances have reality, and reality involves appearances.

I think that, if true, these theses necessitate drastic and illuminating modifications to the *camera obscura* metaphor in ways which I will explain later.

Phenomenal forms and real relations
Before going on to give a detailed account of Marx's use of

this distinction in relation to his analysis of the categories of political economy I will give in this section further clarification and elaboration of Marx's general thesis. The distinction is referred to in *Capital* by a variety of interchangeable terms. Phenomenal forms are called semblances, appearances, estranged outward appearances, illusions, forms, forms of manifestation. Real relations are called essences, real nature, actual relations, secret or hidden substratum, content, inner connections. And the distinction is a systematic one in Marx's later writings. That is to say it is not invoked in an *ad hoc* fashion nor is it appealed to only infrequently. It is involved systematically at each point where the problem of mystification arises, and this in connection with the discussion of many different categories (not *only* in connection with the famous fetishism of commodities). Norman Geras has listed some of its occurrences.[12] His examples, and those given elsewhere in this paper mostly relate to a discussion of basic socio-economic formations, but it is important to notice that the distinction is also used in relation, for example, to the theory of the state and of the class struggle.[13] [14]

> ... the different states of the different civilized countries, in spite of their manifold *diversity of form*, all have this in common, that they are based on modern bourgeois society, only one more or less capitalistically developed. They have, therefore, also certain *essential features* in common. In this sense it is possible to speak of the 'present-day state'. ... (My emphases)

> It is altogether self-evident that, to be able to fight at all the working class must organize itself at home as a class and that its own country is the immediate arena of its struggle. In so far its class struggle is national, not *in substance*, but as the *Communist Manifesto* says, *'in form'*. (My emphases)

And note that in such cases as these Marx is also, as in the cases I will be analysing later, discussing the origin or basis of *ideology* (the ideology of the independence of the state and society in the first case, and that of nationalism in the second).

This distinction between phenomenal form and real relation is applied both to the order of reality and to the order of language and thought ('phenomenal forms appear as modes of thought'). Wages, for example, are an aspect of social reality, namely its phenomenal aspect. And the category 'wages' or 'price of labour' is a conceptual category. One thinks about and talks about social relations in these terms *because* these categories have the same form that reality has, because this is the form in which reality 'is presented to us'. 'Value of labour-power' is both a real relation, the exchange relation between the worker and the capitalist and it is a scientific category in terms of which one understands that real relation. This means that the distinction is not a superficial one, a simple rewording of some such commonsense distinctions as those between 'superficial' and 'profound' or 'confused' and 'clear'. It is a distinction that contains a substantial epistemological theory about the relation between thought and reality and about the origins of illusions about reality. This theory is that the origin of ideological illusions is in the phenomenal forms of reality itself.

This theory is also presented by Marx using the concepts 'imperceptibility', 'invisibility' and related notions. In these terms the theory says that it is a feature of social life, and in particular the life of social production, that it is so structured as to render that social reality sometimes opaque to its participants. The invisibility of real relations derives from the visibility of outward appearances or forms. The apparent immediacy of these forms obscures their mystificatory character. For example, of the commodity-form and of the systematic illusion of individual freedom Marx says

> It is, however, *just this ultimate money-form* of the world of commodities that actually *conceals, instead of disclosing*, the social character of private labour, and the social relations between individual producers. (p. 76)

> A commodity is therefore a mysterious thing, simply because in it the social character of men's labour appears to them as an objective character stamped upon the product of that labour; because the relation of the producers to the sum total of their own labour is *presented to them* as a social relation, existing not between themselves, but between the products of their labour. *This is the reason* why the products of labour become commodities, social things whose qualities are at the same time *perceptible and imperceptible by the senses*. (p. 72)

The Roman slave was held by fetters: the wage-labourer is bound to his owner *by invisible threads*. The *appearance* of independence *is kept up by means of* a constant change of employers, and by the fictio juris of a contract. (p. 574) (My emphases throughout)

In Geras' words then Marx is providing us with an analysis of 'the mechanisms by which capitalist society necessarily appears to its agents as something other than it really is.... It is because there exists, at the interior of capitalist society, a kind of internal rupture between the social relations which obtain and the manner in which they are experienced.'[15] The function of ideology is to keep hidden the real social relations. But the possibility of performing this function is not given in the possibility of some individual wishing to perform this function, or deliberately designing a language, or using a discourse in which it may be performed. Ideological language does not just distract attention away from real social relations, nor does it explain them away, nor even does it directly deny them. It structurally excludes them from thought. And this is because the phenomenal forms of social life constitute not merely a realm of appearances of particulars, but appearances articulated upon a semantic field. Social life is a domain of meanings with which men 'spontaneously' think their relations to other men and to nature. It is therefore not accurately captured in the idealist notion of a 'world-view'.[16] Social life is structured like a language; or rather the conditions that make it possible for social life to be of a particular kind (a particular mode of production) are also conditions for the possibility of a particular language. These conditions are material conditions and are the social practices which constitute a particular mode of production. The 'natural self-understood' meanings encountered in social life form a text which one needs to decipher to discover its true meaning. 'The characters that stamp products as commodities, and whose establishment is a necessary preliminary to the circulation of commodities, have already acquired the stability of natural, self-understood forms of social life before man seeks to decipher . . . their meaning.' (p. 75)

I think that the theory of ideology which I have been presenting can only be clear if it is examined in its application in detailed analyses.[17] Lack of space here means that I will only be able to present sketches of Marx's analyses. I will give four sketches using each as a way of making a general point. I will deal mostly with the wage-form and the money-form but it is important to note that Marx's treatment follows exactly the same lines in relation to all the categories (commodity-form, value-form, etc.) I use mainly the wage-form partly for ease of exposition and partly because of its clear and direct connection with the problem of the dominance of bourgeois ideology in trade union practice.

The mystification of the wage-form

The wage payment seems to involve a fair exchange of equivalents.

> If history took a long time to get at the bottom of the mystery of wages, nothing, on the other hand, is more easy to understand than the necessity, the raison d'être, of this phenomenon. The exchange between capital and labour at first presents itself to the mind in the same guise as the buying and selling of all other commodities. The buyer gives a certain sum of money, the seller an article of a nature different from money. (p. 540)

Marx's argument here depends on his distinction between labour and labour-power. That which is sold by the worker is his labour-power; the capitalist buys the labourer's capacity to work for a certain period of time. The labour performed in that period creates value. It creates as much value as is paid back to the worker as his wage, and it creates value over and above this amount, it creates surplus-value which is retained by the capitalist.[18] Labour itself does not have value.

> Labour is the substance and the immanent measure of value, but has itself no value. In the expression 'value of labour', the idea of value is not only completely obliterated, but actually reversed. It is an expression as imaginary as the value of the earth. These imaginary expressions, arise, however, from the relations of production themselves. They are categories for the phenomenal forms of essential relations. (p. 537)

Imaginary expressions have their home in the ordinary language of everyday life. 'Classical Political Economy borrowed from every-day life the category "price of labour" without further criticism . . . ' (p. 537) 'On the surface of bourgeois society the wage of the labourer appears as the price of labour, a certain quantity of money that is paid for a certain quantity of labour. Thus people speak of the value of labour'. (p. 535) For Marx the fact that people speak of the value of labour, that this is a 'spontaneous, natural' mode of speech under capitalism, shows that 'ordinary language', far from being something to which one should appeal in theoretical discussion, is something which one has good grounds for suspecting of distortion. Ordinary language is the repository of category mistakes. Theoretical discourse corrects ordinary language, tells one what one *should* say. Ordinary language, and the philosophy which makes a fetish of it, has, as Marx says, things standing on their heads.

The fact that the wage-form has the form of an exchange of equivalents, then, disguises the reality which is that wage-labour contains unpaid labour and is the source of surplus-value. One can consider the working day as divided into that period in which the labourer works to create value equivalent to his own needs of means of subsistence, and another period in which he works to create value given *gratis* to the capitalist. One of Marx's criticisms of the Gotha programme was that it had fallen back into the modes of thought of bourgeois ideology on this point and he restates, in his *Critique* his analysis of the real relations involved.[19]

> . . . wages are not what they *appear* to be, namely, the *value*, or *price*, *of labour*, but only a masked form for the *value*, or *price*, *of labour-power* . . . it was made clear that the wage-worker has permission to work for his own subsistence, that is *to live*, only in so far as he works for a certain time *gratis* for the capitalist . . . the system of wage-labour is a system of slavery . . . whether the worker receives better or worse payment. (Marx's emphases)

It is for this reason that the notion of a 'fair wage', another of the imaginary expressions of everyday life, is an absurd one. The very meaning of wages which is now deciphered is the extraction of unpaid labour. Therefore wages are unfair as such.[20]

This particular mystification illustrates a general point, namely that the transformation from real relations to phenomenal forms is a transformation in which a complex relation (or a relation of relations, as in the complex wages-money-value-commodities, etc.) is presented as a simple relation or is presented as a thing or the property of a thing.[21] Thus here an apparent relation of exchange of equivalents is in reality a compound of an exchange of equivalents plus an extraction of surplus-value; and this compound is itself ultimately analysable into a complex set of relations between relations.[22] Also what appears as a fair and free exchange (a contract) is in reality a relation of exploitation and domination.

At this point one can begin (but only begin) to see the connection between ideological categories and ideology in the broader sense, that whole range of discourse and practices structured by these categories. In this familiar case one can see some of the connections between the wage-form and the ideological concept of a fair wage. On the basis of complex comparisons the workers, or the organizations which defend their interests, negotiate wage agreements. The political party which is thought of as that which represents the workers' interests, has as one of its slogans 'a fair day's wage for a fair day's work'; and has attempted to enact an 'incomes policy', a machinery for defending both 'employers' and 'employed' against 'unfairness', thus also defending 'the national interest'. In difficult cases (for example 'special cases') a court of inquiry is empowered to arbitrate and suggest ways of reaching a 'just settlement' which is then 'freely' agreed to by all parties.[23] Now all of this is *necessary*. It is no good ever losing sight of the fact that the workers' fight to defend themselves in such ways is a necessary response to those forces in capitalist society which systematically tend to sacrifice their interest. But it is also true that this historically elaborated complex of institutions and practices is a mystification because it systematically excludes an understanding of real social relations.

Now if it is necessary for the working class to conduct an economic, trades-union struggle in self-defence, and if the spontaneous language in which this struggle is conducted is structured by the wage-form and other 'natural, self-understood' bourgeois categories, and if these categories and their embodiments in practice *systematically exclude* the categories of real relations, then what is the point of saying that the workers *ought not* to be '*exclusively* absorbed' in this struggle?[24]

> [The workers] ought not to be exclusively absorbed in these unavoidable guerrilla fights [against the tendency to decrease real wages, to reduce the working day, etc.] incessantly springing up from the never-ceasing encroachments of capital or changes of the market. They ought to understand that, with all the miseries it imposes upon them, the present system simultaneously engenders the *material conditions* and the *social forms* necessary for an economic reconstruction of society. Instead of the *conservative* motto '*A fair day's wage for a fair day's work!*' they ought to inscribe on their banner the revolutionary watchword '*Abolition of the wages system!*' (Marx's emphases).

If this is not to be a purely idealist moral exhortation there must be some sense in which it is possible to conduct the struggle on the three fronts mentioned at the beginning of this paper, the theoretical, the political and the economic,[25] for it is this that is involved in this passage from Marx. It would be impossible to clarify the issues involved here without a very long detour. I am only concerned to make the point that Marx's theory of ideological categories does not contradict the demand for a three-fold struggle and in fact may actually help to reveal its theoretical basis. How is one to understand the double thesis of Lenin; 'the spontaneous struggle is dominated by bourgeois ideology' *and* 'the working class spontaneously gravitates towards socialism'?[26] And how is it possible in practice to *both* conduct the necessary defence of workers' economic interests and simultaneously struggle for 'economic reconstruction of society'? These problems have been the central theoretical and practical problems for the workers' movement since the debates on reformism in the SDP to the current debates on the alleged reformism of the continental communist parties.

There are two points which would need to be taken into account in this debate which spring directly from Marx's theory of ideology. First, the present system 'engenders the material conditions and the social forms necessary for an economic reconstruction of society'. The system 'real relations/phenomenal forms' is a dynamic one and is not unchanging any more than is the mode of production of which it is an aspect. Second, it does not follow from the fact that the categories of bourgeois ideology exclude socialist categories that the reverse of this is also true. There is a sense in which the wage-form, etc. are included in or assimilated into the categories of *Capital*. I can only indicate here that Marx attempts an explanation of this inclusion in the 1857 Introduction, in the section 'The Method of Political Economy'.[27]

The interdependence of categories

Notice also about the wage-form that it conceals not only the real relation involved in the exchange transaction, but that it also conceals the real nature of the labour-fund, or variable capital, from which the labourer is paid. This particular mystification is analysed by Marx in the section of *Capital* on 'The Accumulation of Capital'. 'The simple fundamental form of the process of accumulation is *obscured by* the incident of the circulation which brings it about, and by the splitting up of surplus-value. An exact analysis of the process, therefore, demands that we should, for a time, disregard all *phenomena that hide the play of its inner mechanism.*' (p. 565) (My emphases). It is worth noting the particular forms of concealment involved here because they illustrate another general point that I want to make explicit, namely that the various appearance-forms are not independent. They support each other. Each form can appear as an element in the composition of any other form; and each element is itself a form constructed out of other elements. It is this that defines the categories as a *structure* of appearances.

In this case one has the following particular combinations. How is it that the source of the wage is obscured? It is because it is paid in the form of *money*. But,

> this money is merely the transmuted form of the product of his labour. While he is converting a portion of the means of production into products, a portion of his former product is being turned into money. It is his labour of last week, or of last year, that pays for his labour-power this week or this year. The illusion begotten by the

> intervention of money vanishes immediately, if, instead of taking a single capitalist and a single labourer, we take the class of capitalists and the class of labourers as a whole. The capitalist class is constantly giving to the labouring class order-notes, in the form of money, on a portion of the commodities produced by the latter and appropriated by the former. The labourers give these order-notes back just as constantly to the capitalist class, and in this way get their share of their own product. *The transaction is veiled by the commodity-form of the product and the money-form of the commodity.* (p. 568) (My emphases)

This example illustrates the point that whichever category one starts with in the immediate problem (in this case Marx is discussing the simple reproduction of capital) this inevitably leads to an analysis in which all the central categories are employed. Their systematic relations in reality are reproduced in their systematic relations in thought. Thus the analysis of the simple reproduction of capital involves the recognition that the capitalist pays the labourer by returning to him only a portion of that which is produced by him. This is obscured by the intervention of money, which makes it seem as if the capitalist has some other source of wealth than the expropriation of unpaid labour. And this intervention of money is an aspect of the commodity-form of production. And the commodity-form of production is that form in which use-values are produced for exchange, and are exchanged in relation to their values. As Marx says, 'the transaction is veiled by the commodity-form of the product and the money-form of the commodity'. Thus the real process is veiled not by some single element but by the whole system of related elements. The bourgeois economist cannot see through the concept of capital as source of the labour-fund because the concept is not the name for a simple empirical relation which can be examined independently. He is caught up in a system of categories which generates 'solutions' to each particular analytic problem in a way like that in which a particular calculation in arithmetic is generated by the whole of arithmetic.

Historical specificity of phenomenal forms
Taking Marx's analysis one step further will demonstrate a

third and extremely important point about the forms of opacity, namely that they differ under different modes of production, they are historically specific. Marx often reveals a real, but hidden, relation in capitalism by reference to other modes of production in which this particular relation or its equivalent is transparent. Mystification can occur, especially at the level of theory (for example political economy) when a correct analysis of some aspect of social relations goes together with the assumption that that form of the relation is a natural one and not an historically specific one. Consider, for example, the fact mentioned above that the labour-fund appears in the form of capital. This is specific to the capitalist mode of production. 'The bourgeois economist whose narrow mind is unable to separate the form of appearance from the thing that appears, shuts his eyes to the fact that it is but here and there on the face of the earth, that even now-a-days the labour-fund crops up in the form of capital' (p. 569). But notice that this 'shutting of the eyes' is not simply a wilful refusal to see a fact. The secret of the labour-fund, namely that it is accumulated surplus-value, *cannot be thought* within the categories of bourgeois political economy.[28] The 'narrow mind' of the bourgeois economist is thus not simply the narrow mind of the bigot or the fool but is, as Marx says, the narrowness of the mind 'which is unable to separate the form of appearance from the thing that appears'.

In order to demonstrate the correctness of his own analysis Marx has simply to refer to an historical example the relation of which to its equivalent under capitalism is made clear *by Marx's categories*; that is it is not made clear by simply referring to the facts in an empiricist sense.[29] Thus,

> Let us take a peasant liable to do compulsory service for his lord. He works on his own land, with his own means of production, for, say, 3 days a week. The 3 other days he does forced work on the lord's domain. He constantly reproduces his own labour-fund, which never, in his case, takes the form of a money payment for his labour, advanced by another person. But in return, his unpaid forced labour for the lord, on its side, never acquires the character of voluntary paid labour. If one fine morning the lord appropriates to himself the land, the cattle, the seed, in a word, the means of production of this peasant, the latter will thenceforth be obliged to sell his labour-power to the lord. He will, *caeteris paribus*, labour 6 days a week as

before, 3 for himself, 3 for his lord, who thenceforth becomes a
wages-paying capitalist . . . from that moment the labour-fund,
which the peasant himself continues as before to produce and
reproduce, takes the form of a capital advanced in the form of wages
by the lord (p. 568).

Money, commodities and language

The conditions for the production of ideology are the conditions for the production of a language, and can only be understood by reference to the structure of forms and social
practices which systematically enter into the production of
particular concepts and propositions in that language.
Ideology is not a collection of discreet falsehoods but a matrix
of thought firmly grounded in the forms of our social life and
organized within a set of interdependent categories. We are
not aware of these systematically generative interconnections
because our awareness is organized through them.

> Whenever, by an exchange, we equate as values our different pro-
> ducts, by that very act, we also equate, as human labour, the different
> kinds of labour expended upon them. *We are not aware of this,
> nevertheless we do it.* Value, therefore, does not stalk about with a
> label describing what it is. It is *value, rather, that converts every
> product into a social hieroglyphic.* Later on, we try to decipher the
> hieroglyphic, to get behind the secret of our own social products
> [that is, the value-form]; for to stamp an object of utility as a value, is
> just as much a social product as language (p. 74) (My emphases).

The puzzle of *money* is especially like the puzzle of
language. Each element, taken by itself (a word, a coin)
seems to have the power to function in an efficacious act
(of reference, of exchange) by virtue of having a particular
property (a meaning, a value). In each case the puzzle derives
from the contrast between the efficacy of the element on the
one hand, and the arbitrariness of its substance (sounds,
inscriptions, bits of metal or paper) on the other. How is it
possible to breathe life into a sign?[30] How is it possible to
conjure value into a coin? The fetishism of commodities
(of the value-system and of the money-form) has its equivalent
in the fetishism of names (of the concept-system and the
reference-form). This is why it is not just a joke to say that
just as money is the universal medium of exchange of labour-

power and commodities so logic is the universal medium of exchange of concepts and propositions. And just as political economy cannot take the money-form for granted but must explain it, similarly philosophy cannot take logic for granted but must explain it.

The arbitrariness of the money-substance (like that of the sign-substance in linguistics) that is the fact that there is no necessary or natural connection between the physical properties and the monetary properties of a coin, has given rise to the mistaken notion that money is a *mere symbol*.

> In this sense every commodity is a symbol, since, in so far as it is value, it is only the material envelope of the human labour spent upon it. But if it be declared that the social characters assumed by objects, or the material forms assumed by the social qualities of labour under the regime of a definite mode of production, are mere symbols, it is in the same breath also declared that these characteristics are arbitrary fictions sanctioned by the so-called universal consent of mankind. This suited the mode of explanation in favour during the eighteenth century. Unable to account for the origin of the puzzling forms assumed by social relations between man and man, people sought to denude them of their strange appearance by ascribing to them a conventional origin. (p. 91)

The parallels between philosophical theories of meaning and economic theories of value should be no surprise because the structural feature that the phenomena have in common is the dislocation between the invisibility of the social life which makes them possible and the visibility of the individual acts in which they enter into social practice.

Ideology and Dialectic

I will recapitulate some of the points that I have been making by returning to the *camera obscura* metaphor. The relation between reality and the representation of reality in men's brains is not a relation involving three independent entities (two entities and a mediating entity between them) as is suggested by the *camera obscura* and the mirror-image metaphors. Marx's metaphor of 'inversion' is notoriously difficult to understand and has suggested many different interpretations. The metaphor continues to occur throughout his later works. It is worth remembering that this very same metaphor of inversion, plus that of reflection, mixed with that of the kernel and its shell, all occur together in the very famous passage in the Afterword to the second German edition of *Capital* in which Marx struggled to explain the difference between Hegel's dialectical method and his own.[31] Hegel's dialectic was the mystified form of the dialectic and was an aspect of the famous 'German Ideology'. Marx's discussion of it is both an attempt to identify his own dialectical method and an attempt to explain the relation between a mystified form of thought and its nondistorted equivalent. But the multitude of interpretations of this passage, and its obvious inadequacy as a theoretical statement (how does one conceive of turning something 'right side up again' in order to discover 'the rational kernel within the mystical shell'?) has lead to an ambitious attempt by Louis Althusser to analyse the specific problem that Marx was struggling with and which lead him back again and again to this metaphor.[32] Althusser's analysis focuses particularly on the problem of Marx's dialectical method. I think that since the metaphors in question are invoked by Marx most often in relation to the general problem of mystification (and not only mystification in its specifically Hegelian form) it would be worth trying to think beyond them here also.

The difference between Marxian categories and the ideological categories of, for example, political economy, is that where the latter designate things and their properties the former designate internal relations and their transformations; and where the latter designate relations between things the former designate relations between relations.[33] This is the most general form of what Marx calls 'fetishism'. For example,

> Whence arose the illusions of the monetary system? To it gold and silver, when serving as money, did not represent a social relation between producers, but mere natural objects with strange social properties. And modern economy, which looks down with such disdain on the monetary system, does not *its* superstition come out as clear as noonday, whenever it treats of capital? How long is it since economy discarded the physiocratic illusion, that rents grow out of the soil and not out of society? (p. 82)

Similarly I think the difference between Marx's theory of

ideology and the ideology of ideology is that whereas the latter thinks of it in terms of two elements and a relation between them (or one element, reality, and its property of creating another element, an idea) Marx's theory is dialectical. It is a theory of a totality. Both the nature of the components and that of the relations between them are thus drastically different. It can be represented as below although it should be remembered that this is presented as merely a helpful graphical device and should not be taken too seriously especially inasmuch as it can give no account of the relations within the totality.

D	REPRODUCTION	A real relations	TRANSFORMATION	B phenomenal forms	PRESENTATION	C ideological categories	GENERATION	D discourse practice (morality, philosophy, religion politics, law)	REPRODUCTION	A
Examples:		labour of production, relations of production		value-form (value adhering to an object, value relations) money-form, etc.		value money commodity etc.		buying and selling, wage-demands, advertising, evaluating, etc		

The properties of this system are complex. I can only make a few comments here by way of highlighting some of its differences from the *camera obscura* model. I have said that this model differs from the earlier one both in the nature of its components (A, B, C etc.) and in the relations between them. In both these respects we can only understand the model by reference to some concept of a structured totality. As Balibar points out[34] the notion of the structural complexity of a totality was introduced by Althusser in order to clarify the relations within the totality base-superstructure, that is the social structure as a whole, as an articulation of several relatively autonomous levels. But it is also true that each of these 'levels' is itself a structured totality. I have given some indication of this above in discussing the interdependence of ideological categories, and below I note briefly a similar feature in relation to the level D, discourse and practice. It is equally true that 'real relation' names (for example social-labour, capital, interest, surplus-value, property) are not the names of things, nor even of relations between things, but of structured functions. In his attempt to grasp this Ollman quotes Marx on 'fixed capital':[35] 'It is not a question of a definition which things must be made to fit. We are dealing here with definite functions which must be expressed in definite categories'.

Thus, relations *within* A, B etc. are not easy to describe. But it is clear that the relations within A are not the same as those within C (the relation between labour and value for example) and that the inversion metaphor, with its preservation of internal relations in the transformation from real to ideological categories, is therefore incorrect. As for the relations *between* A, B etc., it is again clear that, however difficult to describe they may be, certain indications of difference from the earlier model can be made. The problem would be to spell out the properties of the new model in such a way as to preserve certain of Marx's central tenets; in particular the interpretation would have to be compatible with some notion of historical materialism and with the doctrine of the determination in the last instance by the 'economic'. However this is done at least it is clear that, unlike the earlier model, this later one shows that each of the elements A, B etc., is a necessary condition for each of the others. In particular D is necessary for A (which removes the most blatant problem of the 'phantom' metaphor, its suggestion that social reality is independent of 'ideas'). The way in which D relates to A is suggestively analyzed by Althusser in his theory that ideology, as 'materialized' in the Ideological State Apparatuses, secures the reproduction of the relations of production.[36]

Discourse, practice and institutions
What is the relation between C and D, that is between ideological categories and ideological discourse and practices? The massive, powerful presence of mystification secreted by man in the course of his social production and consumption, in its extremely diverse visual, linguistic and institutional forms, is ultimately constructed upon (determined in the penultimate instance by?) the spontaneous categories of the forms of representation of social life. But clearly many

mediations and many local specificities would have to be taken into account in any convincingly detailed analysis of some of the more elaborate or bizarre forms of ideological discourse (religions, moralities, philosophical systems etc.). Also one would have to know how to distinguish in any particular case between superficial, apparent, manifest semantic content, and deeper, more revealing, latent, formative principles of discourse. At the surface level ideology is infinitely flexible and a determined ideologist can plunder even the least likely sources for sentences, images, phrases, words, with which to forge effective weapons (think of Watney's beer and the 'Red Revolution'; or of Nixon at a banquet in Peking invoking the image of the Long March). Such curiosities remind one that meaning is not a matter of words, images, phrases, etc. taken in isolation, but of an order of discourse and practices within which particular words, phrases, or images can take on a variety of meanings. It should also remind one of the problem that discourse is over-determined, so that there may well be levels of relative coherence and intelligibility autonomous from that of any particular set of generative categories. Thus the theory of ideology outlined here is clearly very incomplete inasmuch as it would have to be expanded to include a theory of mediations and over-determination to make of it a useful tool of analysis for cases which are less directly grounded in the particular categories discussed in *Capital* than are those related to the wage-form discussed above.

It must also be remembered that ideology is present in history not as disembodied thought, nor merely in the form of the thought, speech and behaviour of individuals, but in social organizations of various kinds. (See Althusser's concept of Ideological State Apparatus mentioned above.) Since I have been mainly concerned with the cognitive basis of ideology I have no doubt been using rather abstract concepts which may have suggested that phenomenal forms and their corresponding ideological categories exist only as aspects of the cognitive acts of individuals, for example the experience of the individual worker of his wage-transactions and of his production and consumption of commodities. But of course it is not this that is involved at all. The worker's experience is mediated not only by language and culture but also by social institutions. The worker not only reads newspapers and watches television, but is also a member of a family, has been to school, belongs to a union, has perhaps been in the army, and in a football club, is perhaps a member of a church. The conditions for the production of mystification are not abstract but are material and historical.

Keeping this in mind one can get a firmer grip on the problem of the domination of the workers' movement by bourgeois ideology that has been a continuing theme of this paper. Bourgeois ideology dominates because, within serious limits, *it works*, both cognitively and in practice. It provides intelligibility and is embodied in effective working-class organizations. This is the point made by E.P. Thompson in his argument against some of the abstractions of Perry Anderson's analysis of the 'peculiarities of the English'.[37] The main peculiarity diagnosed by Engels was the dominance of unionism over politics, 'the indifference to all theory which is one of the main reasons why the English working-class movement crawls along so slowly in spite of the splendid organization of the individual unions.'[38] Thompson's explanation of this absence of a socialist political and theoretical counterbalance to the spontaneously bourgeois union movement in England consists in locating this absence in the context of the history of the labour movement's success.[39]

> ... the workers, having failed to overthrow capitalist society, proceeded to warren it from end to end. This 'caesura' [between the defeat of Chartism and the appearance of strong unions and eventually the Labour Party] is exactly the period in which the characteristic class institutions of the Labour movement were built up – trade unions, trades councils, TUC, co-ops, and the rest – which have endured to this day. It was part of the logic of this new direction that each advance within the framework of capitalism simultaneously involved the working class far more deeply in the *status quo*. As they improved their position by organization within the workshop, so they became more reluctant to engage in quixotic outbreaks which might jeopardize gains accumulated at such cost. Each assertion of working-class influence within the bourgeois-democratic state machinery, simultaneously involved them as partners (even if antagonistic partners) in the running of the machine ... reformist pressures from secure organizational bases, bring evident returns ... British reformism is strong because, within very serious limits, it has worked.

Conclusion

It would not be possible to account further for the nature of the relation between the subject and the reality that Marx describes in ideological discourse without entering further into the theory of language and the theory of consciousness. But it should be clear that from Marx's thesis some negative points about this relation do emerge, points which are criticisms of other possible theories of ideology. It is not necessary to postulate that any basic role in the generation of ideological discourse is played by subjective and individual agencies such as the desire to deceive, or the deliberate intention to manipulate the beliefs of others in such a way as to protect one's own interests. Nor is it necessary to postulate that ideology need be believed only by the aid of some process of self-deception or refusal or bad-faith. Such existentialist concepts are invoked in order to explain how it can come about that a person believes things which are manifestly contradictory, or believes things which he is in a good position to know are false. But Marx's theory postulates that ideology arises from the fact that the situation might be such as to provide a person with reasons for thinking in terms of categories which necessarily generate falsehood and illusion.

Marx's theory does not assert a merely causal relation between socio-economic reality and ideology. This is the trouble with some of his early formulae, such as the famous 'religion is the opium of the people', inasmuch as they can be interpreted as meaning that ideology functions as a sort of drug which acting on a person's cognitive and perceptual equipment would somehow causally prevent him from seeing what was there to be seen. This is at variance with the *Capital* theory which asserts that the basis of ideology is precisely in its apparent justification by the perceived forms of empirical social reality. So, one must reject the view that ideology has its basis in some sort of defective perception of clearly perceptible facts. For Marx understanding comes not from making good the oversights of others, nor from merely noticing what they had not noticed, but from discovering that which is concealed by the apparent facts, or more accurately by the form of the facts that are directly perceptible in social life. It is the forms of social relations with which one is apparently directly acquainted in experience (value, wages, money, commodities, etc.) that are deceptive. Scientific advance is not so much a matter of discovery as of penetration. And this is achieved by systematic conceptual innovation, that is by theory, which allows us to grasp the hidden coherence of the object.

I am not, of course, denying the reality of self-deception. Nor am I denying that there have been and are many who believe what they believe about social relations because they are aware of the connection between such beliefs and the advancement of their own interests. That is to say that in some way or other beliefs which they regard as justified are fortified or are denied criticism because it is in the interests of that person or group of persons that such beliefs be held. Nor am I denying the obvious truth that there are many who attempt to manipulate others into believing things which they know to be false or into thinking in ways that they know to be mystifying or which simply blunt people's critical faculties in such a way as indirectly to prevent them from arriving at the truth. I have no doubt that such methods of attempted manipulation of people's beliefs are very common, that for example the present (1972) President of the United States and many members of his administration are liars, that they and many others not only lie but use their enormous power and wealth to make as certain as possible that their lies fill the media and penetrate into every corner of the language and of people's minds. But I think Marx's theory is an attempt to account for much more puzzling phenomena than this. Namely that at least in certain historical conditions ideological forms of thought are the 'natural self-understood modes of thought'. The bourgeois ideology that has dominated not only the thought of the bourgeoisie but also the theory and practice for example of the British Labour movement for over a century has clearly not had its origins in the methods or instruments that are now available to and used by the cynical elite of crisis-torn America. Such methods have not normally been necessary. If everyone has been brain-washed then it is by the very forms of social reality itself. It is they, Marx says, that are impressed on our brains. Of course this is not an unchanging or unchangeable state of affairs. But just what Marx's theory of the conditions for the production of mystification can teach us about the conditions for the production of knowledge, and for the production of a non-mystifying social reality, are not questions which I have attempted to answer in this paper.

Notes

1   Lenin, *What is to be Done?* (Moscow 1969), p. 41.

2   *Ibid*, p. 25.

3   *Ibid*, p. 42.

4   For some exhilarating analyses, based on structuralist linguistics, of some of these semiological phenomena see Roland Barthes, *Mythologies* (London 1972).

5   Herbert Marcuse 'Repressive tolerance' in *A Critique of Pure Tolerance*, by Marcuse *et al.* (New York 1965), pp. 98, 110.

6   *The German Ideology*, given for example in Lewis Feuer (ed.), *Marx and Engels, Basic Writings on Politics and Philosophy* (New York 1959), p. 247.

7   One might have added here 'also in relation to the problem of madness' with reference to the work of Foucault, *Histoire de la Folie*.

8   See M. Foucault 'The prose of the world', in *The Order of Things*, ch. 2.

9   C. Lévi-Strauss, *The Scope of Anthropology* (London 1967), p. 41.

10 All quotes from *Capital* are from vol. I of the Moore and Aveling translation (Moscow 1961), and the page references are given in the text after each quote.

11 Henri Lefebvre *The Sociology of Marx* (Harmondsworth 1968), p. 62.

12 Norman Geras, 'Essence and appearance; aspects of fetishism in Marx's *Capital*' *New Left Review* LXV (Jan–Feb 1971), p. 69.

13 *Critique of the Gotha Programme* in Marx and Engels, *Selected Works* II (Moscow 1962), p. 32.

14 *Critique of the Gotha Programme*, p. 27.

15 Geras, *art. cit.* p. 71.

16 The notion of 'world-views' tends to be explained on the model of Gestalt switch experiences of visual perception. Marx's view clearly differs from this in at least this basic respect. The difference between the one 'language' and the other is one which can be explained in terms of appearance and reality, or in terms of the aspect of reality which is its appearance and that which is its hidden substratum. Thus the difference is explained by reference to properties of the object and not solely of the subject and his idiosyncracies. No doubt these considerations would form the basis for an explanation of the way in which Marx's epistemology escapes the problems of idealism and relativism with which I do not deal in this essay.

17 I also think that a full treatment of these problems would require a close examination or Marx's theory of categories given in the 1857

Introduction to the *Critique of Political Economy*, especially the section 'The method of political economy'. This is now available in David McLellan, *Marx's Grundrisse* (London 1971), pp. 33–43.

18 This presentation of the concept of surplus-value is certainly fetishistic in as much as it says of various things (labour-power, commodities) that they *have* value. The relation between labour and value cannot be presented here more accurately for lack of space – it would involve noting at least two movements of totalization (a) the labour of the individual does not *in itself* have a relation to value or surplus-value, but only as a component of the aggregate of social labour. (b) the value of the products of labour is correctly understood only in relation to their multiple appearance both as products and as commodities, and hence their location in the spheres both of production and of consumption. The 1857 Introduction (see note 17) is invaluable in its discussion of the semantic and logical problems involved here. A fuller presentation of these relations would be too complex given the space available but would only strengthen and further support the points I am making in the text. Marx himself often appeals, in passing, to such oversimplified examples for ease of presentation.

19 *Critique of the Gotha Programme, Selected Works*, II, p. 29.

20 Marx points out that wages take a *variety of forms* 'a fact not recognizable in the ordinary economic treatises which, *exclusively interested in the material side of the question*, neglect every difference of form' (p. 543). Marx, being interested also in the practical and cognitive (and hence ideological, political, etc.) sides of capitalism, systematically considers forms as well as contents throughout *Capital*. In chapters 20 and 21 he considers some varieties of the wage-form (time-wages, piece-wages), showing how each conceals real relations and how 'difference of form in the payment of wages alters in no way their essential nature' (p. 552).

21 This is most clearly spelt out by Marx in relation to the commodity-form; see ch. 1, sec. 4, 'The fetishism of commodities and the secret thereof'.

22 See note 18.

23 Some of the connections between ideological categories and ideological moral principles are discussed by Marcuse, *Reason and Revolution*, pp. 280–1 for example:

'If wages... express the value of labour, exploitation is at best a subjective and personal judgment. If capital were nothing other than an aggregate of wealth employed in commodity production, then capital would appear to be the cumulative result of productive skill and diligence. If the creation of profits were the peculiar quality of utilized capital, such profits might represent a reward for the work of the entrepreneur'.

24 Marx, *Wages, Price and Profit* in *Selected Works* I, p. 446.

25 See above, first section of this paper, and the quotes from Engels given in Lenin *What is to be Done?*, p. 28 ' . . . the struggle is being conducted

pursuant to its three sides – the theoretical, the political, and the practical-economic (resistance to the capitalists) – in harmony and in its interconnections, and in a systematic way ... '

26   *What is to be Done?*, p. 42.

27   See Introduction 'The anatomy of the human being is the key to the anatomy of the ape.' I think a clear exposition of the theory in this Introduction would be invaluable. It would show, for example, just how different Marx's theory of categories and of ideology is from, for example, the relativist, idealist Khunian theory of 'paradigms' in which two competing paradigms, in a revolutionary period, *do exclude* one another. It would also show how Marx would be able to give an account of 'justification' in terms of his theory of inclusion and hence escape the irrationalism of Kuhn and the retreat to methodology of Lakatos.

28   See Engels, 'Preface to the second volume of *Capital*' (also in *Selected Works*, I, pp. 470ff, where Engels, using an interesting parallel between Marx's theoretical achievement and that of Lavoisier in chemistry, describes how economists had 'remained in thrall to the economic categories as they had found them' thus making it impossible for them to understand surplus-value. 'Then Marx came forward. And he did so in direct opposition to all his predecessors. Where they had seen a *solution*, he saw only a *problem*.' I think the philosophy of science has a lot to learn from such passages.

29   Since this is such a frequent and powerful aspect of Marx's analyses, and since I have dealt with it so briefly, it may be worth referring to perhaps the most extraordinary occurrences of it – in the chapter on 'The Fetishism of Commodities' Marx goes through a series of five distinct historical variations in the relation between the labour of an individual producer and aggregate of social production, to demonstrate the peculiarities of commodity-production (*Capital*, I, pp. 75–9). Or see pp. 539–42 on slavery (' ... in the system of slavery, where frankly, and *openly, without any circumlocution*, labour-power itself is sold ... ').

30   See Wittgenstein, *Philosophical Investigations*, par. 432 'Every sign *by itself* seems dead. What gives it life? – In use it is *alive*. Is life breathed into it there? – or is the *use* its life?'.

31   *Capital*, p. 19.

'My dialectic method is not only different from the Hegelian, but is its *direct opposite*. To Hegel, the life-process of the human brain, that is the process of thinking, which, under the name of "the Idea", he even transforms into an independent subject, is the demiurgos of *the real world, and the real world is only the external, phenomenal form of "the idea"*. With me, on the contrary, the ideal is nothing else than *the material world reflected by the human mind, and translated into forms of thought*. ... The mystification which dialectic suffers in Hegel's hands, by no means prevents him from being the first to present its general form of working in a comprehensive and conscious manner. With him it is *standing on its head*. It must be turned right side up again, if you would discover *the rational kernel within the mystical shell*.' (My emphases).

32 L. Althusser, *For Marx* (Harmondsworth 1969), especially pt. 3, 'Contradiction and Overdetermination'.

33 A brave effort to explain the peculiarities of a 'philosophy of internal relations' and the consequent difficulties in the interpretation of Marx is made by Bertell Ollman, *Alienation: Marx's Conception of Man in Capitalist Society* (Cambridge 1971).

34 Etienne Balibar, 'The basic concepts of historical materialism' in *Reading Capital*, by L. Althusser and E. Balibar (London 1970), p. 215.

35 B. Ollman, *Alienation*, p. 23. The quote is from *Capital*, II, p. 226. This conception of categories and its elaboration in relation to the basic categories of historical materialism is probably most usefully discussed in Balibar, *op. cit.*

36 L. Althusser, 'Ideology and ideological state apparatuses' in *Lenin and Philosophy and other Essays* (London 1971).

37 E. P. Thompson, 'The peculiarities of the English' in *Socialist Register*, 1965. Perry Anderson 'Origins of the present crisis' in *New Left Review*, XXIII.

38 Quoted in Lenin, *What is to be Done?*, p. 27.

39 E. P. Thompson, *art. cit.*, p. 343. See also p. 342.

'Let us look at history *as* history – men placed in actual contexts which they have not chosen, and confronted by indivertable forces, with an overwhelming immediacy of relations and duties and with only a scanty opportunity for inserting their own agency. . . . An interpretation of British Labourism which attributes all to Fabianism and intellectual default is as valueless as an account of Russia between 1924 and 1953 which attributes all to the vices of Marxism, or of Stalin himself. And one thing which it lacks is any sociological dimension . . .'

The Theory of Ideology in General: A Response to John Mepham's Article
STEVE BUTTERS

JOHN Mepham's article, a most valuable contribution to the developing discussion in Britain about theory and methods for cultural studies within historical materialism, very firmly and lucidly rejects two lines of approach to the Marxist theory of ideology in general: firstly, that which employs the psychology of perception as a metaphorical proving ground for epistemological argument; and secondly, that which refers the structure and effectivity of ideological discourse to its genetic 'source' in the organization of knowledge-production by a class, class-fraction or *bloc*. This refusal of two major strands in the tradition of British Marxist thought, opens a space for original theorizing of the nature, function and mechanism(s) of ideology. Mepham presents his theoretical work as, firstly, an exposition of theses on ideology drawn from *Capital*, secondly, the presentation of a tentative model of ideology's constitution and function, and thirdly, a discussion of both, in which metaphors and analogies are mobilized and and brought into fruitful conjunction. The argument remains at the level of *descriptive theory* in that metaphor and model are not appropriated to a conceptually rigorous problematic, but Mepham claims that his exposition will have advanced the theory of ideology towards stronger explanation. There are, however, three points of tension, or 'discrepancies' in the argument, which, I believe, signal dislocations between its premises and its objectives.

First Discrepancy : Necessity of structured appearance versus contingency of 'mystification'

> The relation between reality and ideology is the cognitive relation.
> That is to say that mystification has its basis in the perception of the

175

apparently intelligible order of social reality by a process of mis-recognition.

The invisibility of real relations derive from the visibility of outward appearances or forms. The apparent immediacy of these forms obscures their mystificatory character.

Mepham correctly situates the constitution of ideology within the interior determinations of the social formation. Ideology arises in the necessary structuring of appearances; its discourse is generated in the conjunction of categories which have sprung 'spontaneously' from phenomenal forms. But he calls the effects of ideology 'mystification' and 'misrecognition', implicitly referring to an absent, alternative mode of consciousness. This absent alternative, thought half suppressed in the explicit argument, is really visible in the organization of his analysis. Despite the complete opacity of bourgeois appearances, Mepham posits the ultimate accessibility of a set of representations of the real relations which for a demystified consciousness will render the 'inner connections/outer forms' complex quite transparent. As Mepham says reality has to present itself formally (that is through appearances); but he looks to a mode of self-presentation of reality which will, exactly contrary to the current mode, render its inner relations immediately apprehensible by generating transparent phenomenal forms, thus solving *practically* the theoretical 'problems' of fetishism. This opposition between mystifying and enlightening representations (though allowable as a shorthand for signalling the differences between ideological and scientific discourse *within thought*) is the leading edge through which the problematic of Man's 'Self-Estrangement' inserts itself, in the form of a critique of ideology as fetishism[1]. Cultural transparency is a utopian image impossible to describe or formulate in concrete terms: it functions as an ethical support to the critique of fetishism, standing in for a social ontology which demands that men reappropriate 'their' world in such a way as to express perfectly mankind's 'essential properties'. Historical materialism conceives of the humanly-constructed world of culture as both non-central (it leases a negotiable space within natural history), and decentred (although man's commitment to transformative labour has made the world, it has been realized under determinate conditions). If I am right in my inference that the problematic of mankind's self-estrangement under-lies Mepham's discussion of the theme of 'misrecognition effects', then his efforts to banish the creating subject from the definition of ideology have been undermined. This has serious consequences for his endorsement of Louis Althus-ser's theses on ideology and the 'Ideological State Appara-tuses' since Althusser specifies ideology's function as the creation of Subjectivity in culture.

*Second Discrepancy :*ᴅ
Spontaneous genesis versus overdetermination

> The origin of ideological illusions is in the phenomenal forms of reality itself.

Much of Mepham's article lucidly presents theses of Marx concerning the modalities through which the categories of ideology are 'given' to men's consciousness through un-mediated, 'spontaneous' emanation from economic struc-tures, so that they directly organize 'current modes of thought'. But towards the end of his article Mepham intro-duces a massive qualification to the linear causality of real relations → phenomenal forms → ideological categories → ideological discourse: 'The massive, powerful presence of mystification . . . is ultimately constructed upon (determined in the penultimate instance by?) the spontaneous categories of the forms of representation of social life.' Ultimately constructed upon? Determined in the penultimate instance? Although ideological discourse is described in the summary model as 'generated' by the categories, in the case of dis-course 'less directly grounded in the particular categories discussed in *Capital*' this generation has to be understood as 'mediated' because it has been overdetermined. But if the discourse of political economy which is the object of Marx's ideology-critique was in some sense 'under-determined' and immediate, can one accept the assertion that the Marxist theory of ideology in general was successfully founded in *Capital*? In any case, the critique of the discourse of political economy was methodologically privileged, in that Marx exposes its ideologicalness by sliding beneath it the text of his emergent scientific theory of the capitalist mode of production.

This procedure can only be applied in respect of well-formed theoretical ideologies, whose imaginary object is directly displaceable by the object of an established scientific theory. Mepham wants to develop the descriptive theorizing of his model by accumulating modifications to the 'paradigm case' of bourgeois and/or common sense political economy, so as to cover the 'mediations' through which are constituted the 'more elaborate or bizarre forms of ideological discourse'. But methods for uncovering the mediations must surely remain haphazard until the theory of ideology has been 'expanded to include a theory of mediations and of overdetermination'.

Freud's overdetermination process was constrained within an already established set of rules governing the ordering of elements within the paths of symptom formation: Mepham's loose association of the Hegelian problem of mediations with Freud's or Althusser's overdetermination concept suggests a more pragmatic conception of methods for ideology-critique.[2] Most pertinently: if ideological discourse is overdetermined, then it has passed through several levels of practice in its constitution, and the articulations between these levels have inscribed in the discourse, symptomatically, the contradictions ('structured in dominance') which those articulations sustain. A discourse which has been generated 'spontaneously' may render reality opaque merely because it is internally consistent: but a discourse which has been over-determined will endow the surface representations of social life with a flawed opacity, inviting a symptomatic reading.

Where several modes of production exist in combination with one another, the conditions under which ideological discourse is formed will certainly ensure that the formation is overdetermined. If most social formations are founded on a complex base, then Marx's treatment of ideology in *Capital* (which assumes that the capitalist mode of production inhabits a concomitantly 'capitalist' form of society) might be interpreted as providing a limiting case, rather than a paradigm case, of the generation of ideological discourse.

Third Discrepancy :
Fetishization of semiotics versus semiotics of fetishization

> Ordinary language is the repository of category mistakes... (it) has things standing on their heads.

> The puzzle of money is especially like the puzzle of language ... The fetishism of commodities ... has its equivalent in the fetishism of names.

Semiotics understands culture as the system of systems for the exchange of signs : it works to recover completely from their concealment the rules of all the discursive practices which produce the discourse embodied in texts; and (for some semioticians) everything on the surface level of phenomenal forms is textual.[3] John Mepham stands close to the semiotic perspective when he defines ideology as structured discourse, and places at the zenith of his system-model 'discourse and practice' (an unexplained shift from 'discursive practice'). Structuralist linguistics is the paradigm of methods for most semiotics ; and concomitantly in Mepham's article, ideological discourse is affiliated with language itself in its genesis and structuration : 'The conditions for the production of ideology are the conditions for the production of a language, and can only be understood by reference to the structure of forms and social practices which systematically enter into the production of particular concepts and propositions in that language. ...'
Although there is some confusion here, arising from the elision between language in general, an historically specific language, and particular language-mediated discursive practices, it seems fairly clear that Mepham understands the pregiven structuredness of ideologies as more or less homologous with the structuredness of language. Now there is a sense in which language itself does induce an alienation effect : it is the grid upon which culture maps itself, providing the potentiality that cultural practice may be reflexive ; and users of language therefore assume that its deepest coding rules are inaccessible to linguistic interrogation, that language bears as its innermost secret the irreducible rationality of a basic matrix of signification-relations. Mepham approves this assumption in his remark on the value of Lévi-Strauss's work in *La*

Pensée Sauvage, and he grounds much of his argument on such an assumption in so far as he takes the concept 'discursive practice' to be unproblematical for his exposition. But the alienation effect of language's secret linguisticity cannot be a puzzle to be resolved in a demystifying critique of the constitution of all languages: semiotics postpones the project of critique in order to make progress with the technical tasks of identifying codes and fracturing the opaque unity of texts. Mepham now leaps ahead of semiotic analysis and calls for the uncovering of ways in which particular (non-discursive?) forms and social practices enter the production of concepts and propositions; but this is to pose again the whole problem of ideology . . .

Against the grain of the semiotic and structuralist motifs in his exposition, Mepham relapses into the theme of fetishism: '. . .it is not just a joke to say that just as money is the universal medium of exchange of labour power and commodities so logic is the universal medium of exchange of concepts and propositions.' The arbitrary nature of concepts-as-names (grounded in the arbitrary nature of the sign itself) now becomes an example of the fetishization of a world which is burdened with ideological discourse; and the 'puzzle of language' makes itself available for resolution through the critique of the naming-fetish or the signifying-fetish, concomitantly with the critique of the commodity-fetish. The transcedence of capitalism would seem here to be associated with the abolition of the concept and the supersession of logic – a sublimely Hegelian vision. Of course this result stems from a mere slip in Mepham's argument, in that he has substituted the 'puzzle of language' for 'the puzzle of ideological language-codes'; but the slip signals an aperture in the architecture of the argument through which the nerve-gas of the fetishism problematic seeps through to paralyze the entire enquiry.

Conclusion

Each of these discrepancies reflects the resistance of the problem of ideology to the historicism and humanism which are inscribed within the pre-Marxist problematic of the relation between Being and Consciousness. John Mepham's article partially identifies a starting point for the theory of ideology in defining (with Althusser) its function as the sustenance of the reproduction of social relations, but fails to delineate the direction of advance for theoretical work with sufficient consistency and clarity. These critical notes have tended to be negativistic because their author is not able to provide an alternative line for theory's 'long march'. But three suggestions for future work may be made as corollaries to the symptomatic reading of the absences and oversights of Mepham's text.

Subjectivity and Individuation

It is not the 'opacity' of representations which induces 'mis-recognition effects' but the orientation to representations of men unable to escape their relation to objects as a subject.

Different ideological conjunctures give rise to variant forms of subjectivity: that of the bourgeois revolution being associated with the doctrines of 'Possessive Individualism', Empiricism, and the separation of civil liberty within the 'private' sphere. There is a need for serious historical study of the variant forms in which 'subjectivization' is installed in cultural life, and their links with forms of character-building on the level of individual biography.

Fetishism

The metaphor of the fetish is compelling, and may have a relevance for cultural studies quite separately from Lukacs's theory of mystification. Stephen Heath has recently indicated the importance of Freud's theory of fetishism in revealing the process by which the individual reader of ideological texts 'refuses the offer' to read symptomatically, and thus partially penetrate the opacity suggested by the unity of its representations.[4] The reader holds at bay the possibilities for producing knowledge in his reading by focusing on the symbolic code only, and finding in this code confirmation of his existing fantasy-formed 'beliefs'. Here is a point of entry for the application of psychoanalysis to the critique of ideological representations in cultural studies.

Development of socialist aesthetics

The Marxist theory of ideology is needed for constructive purposes beyond cognitive 'demystification': it has a direct relevance to the problems of revolutionary practice in art, and the construction of revolutionary aesthetics. Aesthetic analysis goes beyond the critique of ideological discourse for two reasons: artistic practice encompasses and develops its own material base of technique, economic organization etc; and artistic practice works towards the transformation of ideological forms (through a specific practice of intervention) from a site entirely within the ideological instance. Marxist aesthetics is concerned to identify the modalities of revolutionary art within particular conjunctures, and the ways in which its practice transgresses established traditions of code-use and discourse-form.

Although aesthetics may seem a difficult and peripheral terrain on which to test theories of ideology, the politically pertinent ways in which artistic practice exposes the leading edge of an ideological contradiction, together with the stimulus to theoretical work from the exemplary practice of major artists, make this terrain a bridgehead for Marxist cultural practice. In Brecht's words, a Marxist practice of art criticism adequately informed by theory will entail 'the dialectical transformation of the totality of subjects into a permanent crisis, and hence the conception of the age as a "critical period" in both meanings of the term'. The challenge of aesthetics is to transcend merely cognitive models of ideology's functioning; to grasp the articulations between artistic production and politics; to show how artistic innovation and struggle shift the structure of contradictions within ideology. To this challenge the producers of the journal *Screen* have responded with determination and cogency. Their preliminary work promises to lay the basis for considerable advances in the theoretical analysis of ideological production *in its articulations with other practices*, and a more complete theoretical understanding of the role of work in and on ideology within the preparation of conditions for revolutionary transformation of the whole social formation[5].

Notes

1 The critique of fetishism is that of Georg Lukacs. A good critical account is provided in Gareth Stedman Jones; 'The Marxism of the early Lukacs: an evaluation', *New Left Review* LXX. Mepham's discussion of Marx's treatment of ideology in *Capital* is partly inspired by Norman Geras's 'Essence and appearance: aspects of fetishism in Marx's *Capital' New Left Review* LXV, so while the term fetishism is not central in Mepham's exposition, the theme is clearly a strong influence on it.

2 It is debatable whether Althusser's use of 'overdetermination' in his polemical attempt to loosen up rigid communist notions of base-superstructure determinism follows faithfully the key role of Freud's concept in the theoretical and technical practice of psychoanalysis. But the point here is that Mepham very casually associates overdetermination with Sartre's 'problem of mediations' in a way that suggests a vague notion of serialised determinations (an open series) which could not be warranted as a conceptual borrowing from either Althusser or Freud.

3 For an example of the extremist semiotic perspective see Anthony Wilden, *System and Structure* (1972).

4 Stephen Heath, 'Lessons from Brecht', in *Screen*, XV, no. 2 (Summer 1974). This article also provides an excellent account of the 'Subjectivising' function of ideology.

5 See nos. 1 and 2 of *Screen*, XV, especially the articles by Brewster, MacCabe, Heath and Fortini, and the editorials.

Science and Ideology: Critical Comments on John Mepham's Article

KATHRYN RUSSELL

THE distinction between appearance and reality is a very powerful theoretical device and must be understood in order to grasp fully Marx's character as a revolutionary scientist.[1] This relation between appearance and reality is a necessary but not sufficient condition for Marx's distinction between ideology and science. The relation must be filled out with premises from Marx's dialectical materialism before one can fully understand the relationship between ideology and science. The distinction between appearance and reality is both an ontological and epistemological thesis, that is both the world and our knowledge of it can be said to have a certain 'depth'. ' . . . *ontological depth* appears as a condition of the development of the sciences, so that knowledge grows (as well as changes) as new and deeper layers of reality are progressively identified, described, and explained'.[2] Various metaphors and philosophies are used to express this notion of depth. The structuralists,[3] for example distinguish between surface structure and deep structure and suggest that the truths which are sought by science are to be found at the deeper level.

The fundamental opposition between appearance and reality, for Marx, is that the appearance of equality and freedom under capitalism masks a reality of exploitation and suffering. Reality, for Marx, is articulated on the level of classes. For the bourgeois ideologist, the *individual* forms the basic unit of analysis and that individual is directly related to society. For Marx, the level of the individual is mere appearance; the relation between the individual and society is always mediated by one's class.

If one views making a distinction, as Marx does, between

appearance and reality from the standpoint of the history of science, one sees that such a practice has been an important hallmark of scientific progress and increasing theoretical sophistication. Distinguishing between appearance and reality is a *revolutionary* theoretical device because it is an important way to argue against entrenched systems of belief. The following comment by Roy Bhaskar illustrates that the distinction was used with great success during the 250-year-long Copernican Revolution:

> For Galileo, human sense-experience [appearance] depends upon the contingencies of our sense-organs, the aids to them and the beliefs associated with them. There is thus no necessary correspondence between reality and sense-experience. However sense-experience so impresses itself upon our consciousness that it takes an effort to appreciate the possibility of a disjuncture between it and reality. Copernicus made this leap, Galileo praises him for it, and begins the arduous task of bringing the empirical basis of science into line with what reason (theory) has shown must be so.[4]

Not only was the distinction between appearance and reality itself made during the Copernican Revolution, but it was further claimed that there is a special explanatory relationship between the two such that reality *explains* appearance. In the sixteenth and seventeenth centuries, neo-Platonists and radical scientists claimed that attending only to appearance is superficial and wrong. One must go beyond the bounds of common sense, they said, even though the conclusions one reaches are inconsistent with ordinary modes of speaking and thinking. Thus, contrary to common-sense and appearance, the earth is in motion around the sun and the planets have elliptical orbits. Moreover, it was claimed that the various motions of the earth explained the appearance of, for example, the seasons, and the elliptical paths of the planets *explained* their apparent circular motions. With the development of Newtonian science, given its use of the concept of gravity and the atomic theory of matter, people began to accept the notion that for the natural sciences at least, there is a radical distinction between appearance and reality.

Marxist theory is to social science what the Copernicans were to natural philosophy. Indeed, it claims to *be* a science because it *does* make a radical distinction between appearance and reality. As the Copernicans did, Marx claims that one must go beyond common sense which attends only to appearance, the superficial *phenomenal form* of society, and one must achieve a scientific understanding of the *real relations* which are both constitutive and explanatory of society's immediate form.

A distinction between appearance and reality is parasitic on and is intelligible only with respect to a particular scientific theory, in this case a Marxist explanation of the form of capitalist society. It can be made clearer by pointing to an analogous position in the philosophy of physical science. It is common to distinguish between the macroscopic appearance of a table, for example, and its microscopic structure. The macro-properties of the table, its phenomenal form, is that aspect of the table that is immediately perceived and that which conceals its inherent structure. Reference to its microscopic structure, however, not only more adequately captures the physical characteristics of the table, but also explains why it appears solid to us when it is actually composed of spaces and moving electrons. It is wrong to interpret the phenomenal appearance of the table as its most basic structure. The appearance of the table, like the phenomenal form of society, is not basic but must be explained.

To explain the workings of society, it is not sufficient to simply describe the immediate appearance and regard this as a solution. For Marx, its immediate appearance is but a problem; one must discover and describe the processes that generate this superficial form. Just as physics explains the appearance of inorganic matter, Marxism explains the appearance of capitalist society. Thus, the distinction between phenomenal forms and real relations does not merely centre around a dispute over appearance and reality but involves questions concerning the nature of Marxist scientific explanation. In order to understand the revolutionary nature of Marx's method, one should examine his use of the distinction between phenomenal forms and real relations and discuss how the former is *constituted* and *explained by* the latter. This framework can then be applied to the solution of theoretical and practical problems, like the origin and nature of ideology and the development of class consciousness.

Marx uses the abstract premises of the labour theory of

value and the theory of surplus value to illustrate how ideological processes arise and to explain the unscientific nature
of arguments based on the wage system. By making the
Marxist distinction between appearance and reality and by
looking to the contradictions present in the material conditions of society,[5] one should be able to explain why working-
class consciousness remains within a bourgeois framework.
Why is it, as Lenin remarks in *What is to be Done?*, that 'the
spontaneous development of the working-class movement
leads to its subordination to bourgeois ideology'?[6] John
Mepham, in his very interesting article 'The Theory of
Ideology in *Capital*', tries to answer Lenin's question by
formulating a materialist solution to the problem of ideology.

Mepham discusses the dominance of reformist trade-
union consciousness in Britain's trade-union movement and
the failure of the British working class to develop what Lenin
would call an explicit socialist consciousness. Basing
his interpretation on chapter 19 of *Capital*, I, 'The
Transformation of the Value (and Respectively the Price)
of Labour-Power into Wages', Mepham explains that
workers' consciousness remains within bourgeois categories
when it corresponds to the phenomenal form of the wage
system. Mepham's analysis is important because he points out
that to solve the problem of ideology, one cannot presuppose
that workers ignore the real facts, and one must be able to
explain why some workers accept the interpretation of
society offered to them by the capitalists and their allies.
In other words, any explanation advanced must be materia-
listic: people think the way they do because of the conditions
that they face, not simply because of what is told to them.
He shows that it is not merely the dominance of the capitalist
class itself but also the very 'structure' of bourgeois society
that gives rise to the dominance of bourgeois ideology.

His way of capturing Marx's relation between appearance
and reality is to adopt a structuralist methodology which
differentiates between surface and underlying structure.
He claims that ideology is structured discourse which origi-
nates from the opacity of reality, where the forms of society's
appearance mask its generative, underlying relations. He
believes that the key to understanding the dominance of

bourgeois ideology is to be found in the relation of ideology to reality. This relation is both a cognitive and practical one. For Mepham, it is the structure of the capitalist production process itself that is deceptive. The phenomenal form of this reality serves to provide an apparent justification of the evaluation and explanation of society offered by bourgeois ideology.

Mepham locates an important part of the tendency for bourgeois ideology to dominate within the trade unions in the history of the labour movement's success.[7] He claims that bourgeois ideology dominates the consciousness of the working class to the extent that it provides an *apparently* effective explanation of society and guides action. 'Bourgeois ideology dominates because, within serious limits, it works, both cognitively and in practice. It provides intelligibility and is embodied in effective working-class organizations.'[8] He points out that the system of political beliefs implied by bourgeois ideology are used by workers to provide an interpretation of social life and to suggest courses of action. For example, through the use of bourgeois ideology workers acquire a way of understanding how it is that the capitalist profits from their labour – it appears as though the capitalist does not pay them *enough*. Hence, they demand more, 'a fair days pay'.

Mepham's analysis is a good example of the way the distinction between appearance and reality can be fruitfully applied to some theoretical and practical problem, such as the nature of trade-union consciousness. He suggests that bourgeois ideology arises from the complex 'structure' of capitalist society; it acts as a material force by circumscribing workers' actions, channeling them into reformist trade-union activity. His account is fundamentally a structural-functionalist one based on an epistemological thesis concerning the relation between ideology and reality. As a materialist approach to the problem of ideology, Mepham's analysis is both insightful and important. I believe, however, that it is not dialectical enough. I will now present some criticisms of his adoption of the structuralist model as an explication of Marx's theory of knowledge.

In order to develop a dialectical approach to the problem

of ideology, I think it is essential that all aspects of the problem
are stressed. Otherwise, one will reach an incomplete understanding of the nature of our question. Let us characterize
the problem in the following way:

(1) How does bourgeois ideology arise?
(2) What forms does it take?
(3) How does it act as a 'material force' serving to re-
     produce existing relations of production and determine
     their subsequent development?
(4) How can bourgeois ideology be replaced by 'revolu-
     tionary consciousness'?

Many analyses, including Mepham's, fall short because of a
failure to recognize the significance, for Marx, of the importance of (4) How can bourgeois ideology be replaced by
'revolutionary consciousness'? One must account for the
integral and fundamental relationship that the concept of
change has in Marx's philosophy of science. If one's explanation fails to entail an account of how working-class people
might transcend the dominance of bourgeois ideology, then
one has an inadequate description of Marxist science and of
the process of the production of knowledge. The analysis
has to allow for the replacement of old ideas and practices
with new ones.

This approach to the problem of ideology, therefore, has
to be consistent with a genuine Marxist epistemology, or a
theory about the production of knowledge. In this light, the
analysis can be informed by an understanding of current
philosophical literature on theory replacement and conceptual
change. There are two competing 'theories', that is Marxism
and bourgeois ideology. Bourgeois ideology is able to explain
the events in capitalist society to some degree of effectiveness;
but Marxism also offers an effective explanation of society.
Which theory is more adequate? One test of the adequacy of a
scientific theory is its explanatory power and corrective
force.[9] In this manner, Mepham shows Marxism to be the
superior theory. He uses Marxist science to reveal the inadequacies of bourgeois ideology while simultaneously explaining why the latter appears to correspond to reality and to be an
effective guide for action.

Although there is a lot that can be learned from Mepham's

account, his analysis on the whole is inadequate because of the theory of knowledge implied by his structuralism. Mepham is very impressed with the similarities between Marx's thought and that of some sophisticated structuralists like Freud and Lévi-Strauss. Thus, he is very sympathetic with Althusser's and Balibar's attempts to characterize Marxism as a type of structuralism.

> We can only understand the model [of relations within a totality] by reference to some concept of a structured totality. As Balibar points out, the notion of the structural complexity of a totality was introduced by Althusser in order to clarify the relations within the totality base-superstructure, that is the social structure as a whole, as an articulation of several relatively autonomous levels. But it is also true that each of these 'levels' is itself a structured totality. . . . It is equally true that 'real relation' names . . . are not the names of things, but of structured functions.[10]

I believe that Mepham is not critical enough of the Althusserian school. Marxism is indeed similar to structuralism, but it is also very different. Some of these differences can be brought to light by considering what each has to say about the relation between science and ideology.

For the structuralist, science and ideology are 'discontinuous'. Stressing the difference between science and ideology, Mepham claims that bourgeois ideology dominates under capitalism because Marxist science is *structurally excluded* from workers' consciousness. 'Ideological language does not just distract attention away from real social relations, nor does it explain them away, nor even does it directly deny them. It structurally excludes them from thought.'[11] 'The secret of the labour-fund, namely that it is accumulated surplus-value, *cannot be thought* within the categories of bourgeois political economy.'[12] Now I think it is obvious that something has gone wrong with Mepham's analysis here. To say that bourgeois ideology is constituted by the phenomenal forms in such a way that Marxist categories *'cannot be thought'* fails to allow for *change* of consciousness. In my view his notion of structural exclusion is too strong, is self-refuting and open to obvious counter-examples. Contrary to Mepham, it is not that ideas corresponding to the real relations cannot be thought, but that they are thought in a confused way.

Mepham makes too sharp a distinction between science and ideology. This is consistent with the work of Althusser, Balibar and Bachelard: 'Gaston Bachelard is perhaps best (or even only?) known to English readers as a result of Louis Althusser's systematic use of the concept of an "epistemological break" in this attempt to register the radical discontinuity between Marx's science of history and the ideologies that preceded it.'[13] All these philosophers argue that science is to be sharply distinguished from everyday thought and activity. They argue that it is 'science' which penetrates to the real structure of things and explains how it is that society appears as it does. Ordinary thought is mystifying and must be corrected by rigorous scientific theories. 'Sciences are born by breaking with these (ordinary) modes of thought and they progress discontinuously by further breaks, or recastings of knowledge, in which the epistemological obstacles secreted by these modes of thought must be overcome'.[14]

I would argue, however, that although they are indeed radically different and perhaps discontinuous in some respects, science and ideology are also in some important sense *continuous*. In the 1930s, when the accepted view in philosophy was that scientific progress occurred in a linear, monistic and cumulative fashion and that science was simply a refinement of common sense experience, it was revolutionary to assert that progress occurs with qualitative leaps and bounds and that science and common sense are 'discontinuous'. Carrying these notions to their logical conclusions gave us Feyerabend and his notion of 'incommensurability', that is that the replacing theory was so radically different from the theory that was being replaced that the two were not capable of being compared. But 'incommensurability' has not been a fruitful concept; being basically unintelligible and vague, it has all but been abandoned. Now, in the 1970s, one must retrace one's steps and determine how science and commonsense are continuous because scientific growth and progress are unintelligible without *some* concept of continuity and unity.[15] The concept of a sharp rupture between the consciousness of working people and the 'knowledge' of the Marxist 'scientist' entails that the political consciousness of the working class cannot and could not contain adequate instruments for the *acquisition* of knowledge. It is not my thesis, of course, that there is no difference between science and ideology, but that the distinction cannot be built on the notion of an 'epistemological break'.

To me, the notion of science being simply discontinuous with ordinary modes of thought is one-sided. A dialectical treatment of the problem of ideology will recognize not only the difference between ideology and science but also the similarity between the two. An approach to the problem must incorporate the dialectical relationship between unity and difference.

> It is characteristic of the entire crudeness of 'common sense', which takes its rise from the 'full life' and does not cripple its natural features by philosophy or other studies, that where it succeeds in seeing a distinction it fails to see a unity, and where it sees a unity it fails to see a distinction. If 'common sense' establishes distinct determinations, they immediately petrify surreptitiously and it is considered the most reprehensible sophistry to rub together these conceptual blocks in such a way that they catch fire.[16]

Mepham's talk of structural exclusion is inadequate because it is not sufficiently dialectical. Although one cannot fail to see a difference between science and ideology, one should not prevent oneself from seeing the unity between the two.[17] Analogously, although I have stressed the revolutionary nature of Marx's distinction between appearance and reality, I also want to recognize that, for Marx, appearance and reality are in some important sense the same. Appearance is, after all, part of reality. 'Actually, essence (reality) includes appearance but transcends it in every direction in which what is apparent acquires its importance.'[18] If one stresses the difference between ideology and science as well as appearance and reality at the expense of understanding the unity between them, one cannot account for change and progress and one fails to realize the origin and nature of class consciousness.

Another reason for not wanting to distinguish too sharply between science and ideology is that such a view is tantamount to adopting elitism. It is a symptom of the isolation of radical intellectuals from working people and an all too familiar underestimation of workers' ability to understand their own oppression. This elitism is a manifestation of the fact that our conception of Marxist science is wrong. It indicates that one has not seen the unity between theory and practice, or science and class struggle. Mepham, for instance, views science as conceptual penetration. 'Scientific advance is not so much a matter of discovery as of penetration. And this is achieved by systematic conceptual innovation, that is by theory, which allows us to grasp the hidded coherence of the object'.[19] Mepham's view of science as conceptual penetration combined with his notion of structural exclusion is inconsistent with the fact that, for Marx, theory and practice are *internally related*. If one reduces Marxist scientific activity to conceptual theorizing, one divorces it from its subject matter. Marxist theory is not an activity independent of either the political practice or the conceptual framework of the working class.

Notes

1   I would like to express my indebtedness to Bill Russell and John McEvoy for their invaluable support and for the intellectual stimulus they provided me during the course of many long discussions on the problem of ideology and related issues. I would also like to thank the following people for their helpful comments on an earlier version of this paper: Harriet Applegate, Ron Applegate, Mary Elizabeth Brenamen, Gregg Corr, Alison Jaggar, Bob Moore, Bertell Ollman, Diana Porter, and Ken Ray.

2   R. Bhaskar, 'Feyerabend and Bachelard: two philosophies of science', *New Left Review* 94 (Nov.–Dec. 1975), p. 47.

3   'Structuralism' is a loose concept and is used very differently by different people. Naive structuralists make no distinction (or an insignificant one) between appearance and reality; American structuralism is usually of this type. The more sophisticated structuralists do make such a distinction, for example Lévi-Strauss, Piaget, and Freud. See Miriam Glucksmann, *Structuralist Analysis in Contemporary Social Thought, A Comparison of the Theories of Claude Lévi-Strauss and Louis Althusser* (London 1974), especially ch. 1. European Marxists led by Althusser use a type of structuralism to characterize Marx's thought, an attempt which is illustrative but, to many Marxists, 'insufficiently dialectical'. How one differentiates between sophisticated structuralism, Althussereanism, and Marxian dialectics with its doctrine of internal relations is an interesting theoretical problem. See Bertell Ollman, *Alienation: Marx's Conception of Man in Capitalist Society*, 2nd edn. (Cambridge 1976).

4   R. Bhaskar, *op. cit.*, p. 44. The first parenthetical remark is mine. See also, R. Bhaskar, *The Realist Theory of Science* (1975; 2nd edtn., Hassocks 1978). The emphasis on 'reason' made in this quote should not be foisted directly onto Marx's thesis, however, without serious consideration. The emphasis is an expression of Galileo's rationalism. As an anti-empiricist, Marx does have certain affinities with rationalist thought but these need to be identified.

5   Strategic considerations about practical matters come to the foreground only on a low level of abstraction. To reach this low level of abstraction, subsidiary hypotheses must be added to the abstract theoretical premises. If the question at hand is trade-union strategy, the additional hypotheses should concern (among other things) specifications about present conditions in the trade unions, the history of the trade-union movement, and past and present communist and activist trade union practice.

6   V. I. Lenin, *What is to be Done?* (Moscow, 1969), p. 42.

7 See E. P. Thompson, 'The peculiarities of the English', *The Socialist Register* (New York 1965).

8 Mepham, 'The theory of ideology in *Capital*' (in this volume).

9 See P. K. Feyerabend, 'Explanation, reduction and empiricism', *Minnesota Studies in the Philosophy of Science*, H. Feigl and G. Maxwell (eds.) III (Minneapolis 1962), pp. 46–52; and K. Popper, The aim of science', *Ratio*, I (1957), pp. 29–35.

10 Mepham, p. 163.

11 *Ibid*, p. 152.

12 *Ibid*, p. 159.

13 Bhaskar, *op. cit.*, p. 47.

14 *Ibid*, p. 47, my emphasis.

15 Developing a dialectical approach to the problem of scientific progress and conceptual change is an important task for Marxist philosophers of science. What is needed is some 'synthesis' of the discontinuity/continuity thesis which is not one-sided and does not lose the insights of each approach. In addition to the articles mentioned in footnote 9, a relevant bibliography would include: T. Kuhn, *The Structure of Scientific Revolutions* (Chicago 1962); I. Lakatos, 'Falsification and the methodology of scientific research programmes', *Criticism and The Growth of Knowledge*, I. Lakatos and A. Musgrave (eds.) (Cambridge 1970), pp. 91–196; L. Laudan, *Progress and Its Problems: Towards a Theory of Scientific Growth* (Berkeley 1977); E. Nagel, *The Structure of Science: Problems in the Logic of Scientific Explanation* (New York 1961); and K. Schaffner, 'Approaches to reduction', *Philosophy of Science*, XXXIV (1967).

16 Marx, 'Die Moralisierende Kritik und der Kritisierende Moral', *Werke*, IV, p. 339, quoted in Ollman, *op. cit.*, p. 265–6.

17 This unity is what Althusser directly denies because he rejects a (Marxist) version of the Hegelian notion of supersession (*Aufhebung*).

'...it is precisely the substantial continuity of a process containing its own future *in germ in its own interiority* which is in dispute here. Hegelian supersession presupposes that the later form of the process 'is' the 'truth' of the earlier form. But Marx's position and his whole critique of ideology implies on the contrary that science ... constitutes *in its very meaning* a *rupture* with ideology and that it sets itself up in *another terrain*, that it constitutes itself *on the basis of new questions*, that it raises *other questions* about reality than ideology, or what comes to the same thing, it *defines its object* differently from ideology. ... If we want a historical predecessor to Marx in this respect we must appeal to Spinoza rather than Hegel'. Althusser, *For Marx* (New York 1969) p. 78, n40.

For a defence of the doctrine of internal relations, see Ollman, *Alienation*, 2nd edn., especially Appendix 2.

18 Ollman, *op. cit.*, p. 63.

19 Mepham, *op. cit.*, p. 168.

If you would like to receive regular news on Harvester Press publications, please just send your name and address to our Publicity Department, The Harvester Press Ltd., 17 Ship Street, Brighton, Sussex. We will then be pleased to send you our new announcements and catalogues and special notices of publications in your fields of interest.